Michael McIntosh

SHOTGUNS & SHOOTING
THREE

SHOOTING
SPORTSMAN

ISBN 978-0-89272-776-6

5   4   3   2

www.shootingsportsman.com

Distributed to the trade by National Book Network

Library of Congress Cataloging-in-Publication Data

McIntosh, Michael.
 Shotguns and shooting three / Michael McIntosh.
   p. cm.
 ISBN 978-0-89272-776-6 (hardcover : alk. paper)
 1. Shotguns. I. Title.
 SK274.5.M395 2008
 799.2028'34-dc22

                              2008039088

CONTENTS

INTRODUCTION

When I assembled *Shotguns and Shooting* in 1993 I had no anticipation of a second volume. *More Shotguns and Shooting*, published in 1998, took me almost as a surprise. It just seemed the right thing to do at the time. The stories were there, almost begging to be put into book form, so that I did. That the pair should become a trilogy never crossed my mind—and yet here is *Shotguns and Shooting Three*. I hope you find this one as satisfying as you have the others.

Readers have told me time and again that they find these books both informative and entertaining, which touches upon two of the cardinal reasons why I write at all. Plying the craft of words has been a fascination, possibly even a compulsion, since before I could read. Take it away and I wouldn't know what else to do. Leave it with me and I'll keep on until my last breath. I don't think writers are allowed the privilege of retirement.

Citing everyone who has contributed to the fabric of this book would take up page after page. To them I will simply say that you know who you are and know as well that you have my undying thanks. Three, however, deserve special thanks—Chris Cornell, for giving this a shape, Lynda Chilton, for giving it a look, and Michael Steere, for seeing it into print. Any writer who thinks he can get along without an editor, a designer, and a production manager is playing himself for a fool. I trust I'm not that kind of writer.

From the cornfields of Marion County, Iowa
July 2008

1

FROM THE
STONE AGE

Look far enough back at our lovely sport of shooting on the wing and the guns we use for it, and you'll find two of the most fundamental truths of history: Everything begins somewhere, and nothing evolves except through mutual influence with something else.

In our case, of course, it began with the gun, with the matchlock and the wheellock, with the arquebus, caliver, musket, and all the other forms known generically as "hand gonnes." But through the first phases of development, from early in the fifteenth century until late in the sixteenth, the sport that would later be known as the art of shooting flying remained instead the art of shooting sitting.

The substantial lapse of time between the trigger and the bang, whether the mechanism lowered a smoldering fuse to a priming pan or set a serrated wheel spinning against a chunk of pyrite, so dimmed the chances of hitting an object flying at any angle other than straight away that few gunners even bothered to try.

The change began about 1570 in The Netherlands, where gunmakers devised the snaphaunce lock. It combined the best features of the older systems with the new notion of igniting a powder charge through a striking action, the same concept on which firearms are still made. In the snaphaunce, it involves a chunk of flint gripped in the jaws of a cock. When the sear is tripped, a stout mainspring drives the cock forward, rotating on its axis, so that the flint strikes a steel plate variously called the hammer, steel, battery, or frizzen and showers sparks into a small pan of priming powder. The flash from this passes through a small vent in the side of the barrel and ignites the powder charge inside.

By the time the new system reached the full extent of its evolution, it not only represented the first truly great age of the sporting gun, but also in great measure established the form of the classic gun as we know it today.

The process took just over two hundred years, and at first, the various stages overlapped. While Spanish makers developed the Miquelet lock, English craftsmen working along similar lines devised the Jacobean or dog lock. In both, the frizzen and the flash pan cover, separate parts in the snaphaunce, are combined in one piece. These locks formed the main transitional step between the snaphaunce and the true flintlock, but both were applied almost solely to military arms. By bringing the snaphaunce to its highest level of perfection, the Italian makers of the Val Trompia were the first to turn out sporting guns quick firing enough to be effective against a flying target.

The new sport found its way to France early in the seventeenth century, and there, during the time when France under The Sun King Louis XIV was the most influential country in Europe, both the true flintlock gun and the art of *tir au vol*, shooting on the wing, were established.

Although English makers soon adopted the gunlock in its French form, wingshooting took a relatively long time to cross the English Channel and might have taken even longer but for a chain of events that began in 1642, when civil war broke out between Englishmen loyal to the monarchy and the Puritans who supported a parliamentary form of government. Under Oliver Cromwell's leadership, the Puritans eventually gained the upper hand, beheaded King Charles I in January 1649, and established the Commonwealth of England. Two years later, when Cromwell's army defeated the last Scottish troops loyal to Charles II, the king fled to exile in France.

The Commonwealth lasted until 1653, at which time Cromwell established a military Protectorate and declared himself Lord Protector. He died in September 1658, succeeded by his son Richard. Public support for the Protectorate was already wearing thin, and the younger Cromwell's incompetency proved to be the last straw. In 1660, General George Monk seized control of the government, forced the Lord Protector's resignation, and established a new Parliament which promptly restored the monarchy and invited Charles II to come home and take the throne.

Interest in sport does not usually flourish in times of political and social turmoil, and the Puritans weren't noticeably fond of such pursuits anyway, so it's easy to see why sporting guns and the uses thereof got short shrift in England through the 1640s and '50s. But among the things Charles and his Royalist nobles brought back from France in May 1660 were slender fowling pieces built in Italy, France, Spain, and Germany and a keen interest in shooting birds on the wing.

This novel new approach caught on immediately and to such an extent that owning a fine gun and practicing the art of wingshooting soon became a requirement for any man who aspired to the status of a gentleman. Apparently, though, it was a time more characterized by enthusiasm than great success. As Mr. Markland wrote in his 1727 pamphlet *Pteryplegia: or the Art of Shooting Flying*, English shooters weren't quite as skillful as those in France, "it being as rare for a professed Marksman of that Nation to miss a bird as for one of ours to kill."

Whatever the reason behind such lackluster shooting, it wasn't for want of good guns, for the English trade had been quick to adopt the lightweight, well-balanced form of the European shotguns, and by the beginning of the eighteenth century, English makers had matched and then surpassed the quality of work turned out by their counterparts on the Continent. From the hindsight of history, it's no exaggeration to say that the reign of Queen Anne, 1702 to 1714, marked the beginning of the greatest age of gunmaking the world has ever known, an age that culminated with the perfection of the modern shotgun almost two hundred years later.

The first fifty-odd years went toward refinement rather than invention, as the gun trade concentrated solely upon achieving the highest standards of fit and finish and perfecting the details of their craft. Mechanically, the standard gunlock remained unchanged from the pattern developed in France during the previous century. To see what this involved, spend a moment on the drawings.

The true flintlock uses a one-piece battery/pan cover usually called the frizzen, the tail of which bears against a V spring called the feather spring, fastened to the outside of the lockplate. The lockparts themselves, sear, tumbler, mainspring, and sear spring, are held to the inside of the plate by a bridle, which provides support to the moving parts and at the same time minimizes friction. The tumbler's axis protrudes through a hole in the plate, and the cock is fastened to it with a screw. Internally, the arrangement is essentially the same as you'll find in a modern hammerless sidelock.

Although English gunmakers made no mechanical changes in the flintlock during the first half of the eighteenth century, they made enormous improvements in the craftsmanship by which the locks were built, improvements that serve to show how important even the smallest details of a best-quality gun really are. Screws, for instance: No matter how carefully lockparts are made and fitted, they cannot function any better than the screws that hold everything in place. If the threads are poorly cut and the screws themselves made of soft metal, they soon bend and loosen under the stresses of parts moving by spring tension and when that happens, the whole lock goes out of whack.

Similarly, a lock only works as well as the springs that power it. If they're poorly made or not properly tempered, they won't last long. In a flintlock, main and feather springs must be perfectly balanced with one another. If the mainspring is too light and the feather spring too heavy, the cock can't strike hard enough to snap the pan cover open or create an adequate spark; if both are too heavy, the flint simply shatters.

These and other such procedural matters as case hardening lock parts and plates, using new and better steels, improving the process of tempering springs, and generally paying close attention to perfecting fit and finish were the gun trade's main occupation through the early eighteenth century. During this time, makers began fastening barrels and stocks together with flat, tapered steel bolts rather than the round pins used earlier. Because the bolts could be drawn out without the use of a punch, this made guns easier to take apart for cleaning and lessened the chances of damage to the wood.

Aesthetically, the taste of the day called for rather elaborate decoration and the use of silver for mounts and furniture rather than steel or brass.

Side plates, which in single-barreled guns are fastened to the side opposite the lock and support the screws that hold the lock in place, were typically carved in leafy, floral patterns. Trigger guards and buttplate tangs usually ended in floral- or acorn-shaped finials. Inlay and carving in both wood and steel were common.

The names of the finest gunmakers at work in England during the reigns of Anne and the first two King Georges are not now well known, but they deserve recognition. The efforts of such men as Lewis Barbar and his son James, Henry Delany, James Paul Freeman, and Joseph Griffin paved the way for the generation of craftsmen who would bring the flintlock to its highest form.

The gathering wave of inventive energy started to break at mid century, beginning with the "waterproof" lock. I add the quotation marks because no flintlock, with its external priming pan, can ever be completely sealed against moisture's insidious invasion. Sheer humidity can cause misfires. Still, there's no doubt that the English gun trade came up with some ways of making a flash pan about as water resistant as it could possibly be.

The standard approach was to drill a drain hole at the bottom of the flash shield or fence so that raindrops sliding down the frizzen could keep on going rather than accumulate between the fence and the pan, ready to spill into the primer the instant the cock knocked the pan cover open. And the cover itself was formed oversized with a downturned lip on three sides so it fit over the pan like the lid of a box. Birmingham makers Thomas Noon, Robert Prettyman, and Emanuel Heaton took this to its ultimate conclusion after the turn of the next century by adding a leather gasket, but for the most part the drain hole and overlapping cover remained the most effective means of keeping a priming charge reasonably dry.

More important, however, were two improvements in lockwork that appeared more or less simultaneously in the early 1770s. Both enhanced the flintlock's mechanical efficiency by reducing friction and thereby increasing the speed at which the lock could work. One was the notion of placing a roller bearing at the contact point between the flash pan cover and the feather spring. This not only increased lock speed, but also encouraged stronger sparks off the flint, which in turn made ignition more reliable. Some lockmakers fastened the roller to the pan cover tail while others pinned it to the feather spring. Either way seemed to work equally well.

The other change sought to minimize friction between the long arm of the mainspring and the tumbler. Perhaps someone tried a roller here, too, but the classic solution proved to be a swivel, pinned to the tumbler at one end and shaped in a T at the other. The end of the spring, filed to a double claw hook, fits over the swivel's cross bar, linking the two parts in such a way that friction is virtually nil.

Neither of these innovations came into wide use until the 1790s, but from then on they were standard features of all best quality guns, and they played significant roles in making the flintlock as fast and efficient as it ever got to be. The improved feather spring and frizzen arrangement naturally went obsolete when the caplock took over, but the tumbler swivel is still part of best-quality English-style sidelocks.

Change followed hard upon change. Better manufacturing methods created more efficient powders, allowing gunmakers to shorten barrels from the 42 to 48 inches needed earlier to give the old, slow burning powder time to work up maximum thrust. After about 1760, more and more of the barrels themselves were made in England rather than imported from Spain. Joseph Griffin of Bond Street, London, recognized as the finest gunmaker of the day, was one of the first English barrelmakers, certainly the first great one, and also one of the first English makers to turn out best-quality side-by-side doubles.

Tastes in woodwork changed as well. The older style of stocking single barrels to the muzzle began to give way to more graceful half stocks. Buttstocks grew slimmer.

And a new generation of gunmakers began to emerge. John Fox Twigg succeeded Griffin as the most celebrated craftsman of England. Others turning out first-quality work in the latter eighteenth century included Edward Bate; the two William Jovers, father and son, who worked in partnership with Bate for a few years after about 1805; John Probin; Joseph Heylin; William Wilson; John Bennett; Durs Egg, who founded a gunmaking dynasty; and Harvey Walklate Mortimer, who did the same.

The most important invention of the time, and one of the most important of all time, for muzzle-loading arms came from Henry Nock, who in April 1787 obtained a patent for a new and revolutionary style of breech.

The original means of breeching was simply a flat-faced, threaded steel plug that closed off the rear end of a gun barrel. With the powder charge occupying the full diameter of the bore, ignition through a flash hole involved setting fire to a corner of it, so that a noticeable amount of time elapsed before the full charge was alight. Having succeeded in speeding up the locks, gunmakers soon saw that ignition needed some hastening as well.

First they tried the chambered breech, which amounted to a plug with a funnel shaped cavity. Ironically, this slowed the overall process even further: The powder ignited more efficiently, but the priming flash had to travel farther to reach the tip of the funnel. Nock's solution was to add a sort of antechamber that allowed a small quantity of powder to rest close to the flash hole. This ignited very quickly, sending a jet of flame forward through a narrow channel into the very center of the main charge.

Nock's breech was a seminal breakthrough in gun design. Other makers came up with some patentable variations, all based on Nock's fundamental concept, but no one ever was able to truly improve it. By 1790, the stage was set for the flintlock's final phase of perfection.

Twigg died that year, and his place at the pinnacle of the English gun trade was soon occupied by his erstwhile shop foreman, John Manton, who had left Twigg's employ in 1781 to go into business on his own at 6 Dover Street; the company remained at that address until it closed down in 1878. John Manton took on his younger brother Joseph as an apprentice about 1780. Joseph in turn went on his own in 1793, first in Davies Street, then in Hanover Square, in Oxford Street, and after his first bankruptcy in 1826 at a variety of premises occupied only briefly.

Joseph eventually superseded his brother as the premier English maker, described by Peter Hawker as "the greatest artist in firearms that ever the world produced." Although their personal relationship was marred by rivalry and conflict, the two Mantons influenced English gunmaking in ways impossible to overestimate. Neither contributed much by way of invention, though each obtained several patents and Joseph gets credit for being the first to install an elevated top rib to a double gun, but together they established once and for all a standard of craftsmanship in which perfection was the only acceptable level of quality. To see where this eventually led, we need only consider the names of some craftsmen who either apprenticed or worked in Joseph Manton's shop: James Purdey, Thomas Boss, Charles Lancaster, Joseph Lang, and William Greener. In fact, the only gunmaker to earn a place at the very top of the London trade who didn't train with the

Mantons or one of their proteges was Harris Holland. The Mantons virtu-ally defined the form of the shotgun as well as the standard of workmanship that went into it. John Twigg was mainly responsible for beginning the trend toward less flamboyant decoration, which the Mantons fostered and passed along to succeeding generations.

Essentially, this amounted to a trend toward letting the inherent grace of the gun itself be the primary source of its beauty; of using steel rather than silver or brass for mountings and filing them to simpler shapes; of sleek, straight, checkered stocks finished without carving or inlay; of engrav-ing lockplates in subtle, elegant designs.

Further improvements in gunpowder made 30- or 32-inch barrels truly practical, which in turn meant that the double gun could be built with larger bores and still be lightweight and dynamic in handling.

All in all, it's fair to say that the style and form of the English best gun was established for all time by about 1820, just at the end of the flintlock era. Great mechanical changes lay ahead, first the caplocks and then the breechloaders, but it's important to recognize what didn't change. Take a best-quality sidelock gun built any time since about 1890, anywhere in the world, and look past the hammerless locks, the ejectors, the single triggers, and other such refinements. What you'll see is an English gun as it came to be when guns were fired by flakes of stone.

2

SISTERS IN THE WOOD

Show me a pair of best-quality guns, nestled like elegant lovers in an oak and leather case lined with felt the color of leaves or old, dark wine, and you show me the perfect artifacts of gunning's Golden Age.

They may be as old as grandfather tales or new as the last full moon, but in spirit they belong to a time a hundred years gone, a time when the tides of history conjoined as never before or ever since nor ever will again. It was a phenomenon of the kind historians dream about; social political, and technological currents flowing together at the one time and place where human events were destined to pause, where implications could play out in a long caesura between shocks of cataclysmic change.

England, approaching the last quarter of the nineteenth century: Victoria, gloomy and censorious, had reigned for more than a generation over the greatest empire the world ever knew and over a social system in which the uppermost class enjoyed almost limitless wealth and privilege; the railroads

---

had only recently opened ready access to the game-rich rural areas of an island nation somewhat smaller than Colorado; and the London gun trade owned the most skillful craftsmen on earth.

At the center of it all stood Albert Edward, Prince of Wales, Victoria's eldest son, heir to the throne and arbiter of fashion, born in 1841 and doomed for sixty years to have absolutely nothing to do except what pleased him.

What pleased him most was shooting. He possessed neither the physical capacity nor the taste for hunting, an exercise performed on horseback at breakneck pace in pursuit of hounds in pursuit of a fox. He cared equally little for walk-up shooting with dogs, which had been the standard approach at the time of his birth, but in the 1860s, probably somewhere in Norfolk or Suffolk, someone hatched the idea of having birds flushed and driven toward the guns. With that, the man who would later reign as King Edward VII became the seminal figure in a phenomenon that would ever after influence the nature of shooting and the nature of gunmaking worldwide.

Because his mother steadfastly refused to allow him even the smallest role in public affairs, the Prince was free to follow his own whims; because humorless Victoria took no interest at all in the London social scene, the class to whom the social season was life itself yearned for someone to assume social leadership; because the Prince was as energetic as the Queen was grim, he was happy to oblige; because the Prince chose to spend the autumn and winter shooting in the English countryside, now only a few hours' trip by train from London, society went shooting, too.

It became the great age of country estates and elaborate shooting parties; so elaborate, in fact, that shooting contributed to more than a few bankruptcies, notably those of the Sixth Lord Walsingham and the Indian Prince Victor Duleep Singh. Its heyday lasted nearly two generations, until the beginning of the Great War, and it represented something that has never existed at any other place or time in the history of the world: an entire social system organized around the sporting gun.

And not just any gun, but rather the best gun human hands could make: superbly built, exquisitely decorated, perfect to the last detail. When the wealthiest social class of the most powerful nation on earth went shooting with its future king, nothing less would do and price was no object. That it should be a London gun went without saying, for so far as the British nobility were concerned, London was the only source for the best of anything.

The gun trade naturally was willing to satisfy the demand. As London had always been the political, financial, and social center of the Empire, the most ambitious and highly skilled craftsmen were there already, heirs to a standard of quality established nearly a century before by the incomparable brothers Manton and fostered thereafter by James Purdey, Thomas Boss, James Woodward, Harris and Henry Holland, and others of lesser name but equal skill. From about 1870 until the beginning of the 1914 war, no country in the world could boast as many makers able to supply guns of the absolute best quality, and no city owned more of them than London. Out of it came the finest guns ever built, guns that still represent the standards by which guns everywhere are judged.

In the days when guns were loaded from the muzzles, sportsmen found good reason for using more than one at a time. Even in walk-up shooting a man could enhance his enjoyment just by trading his empty gun for one fully charged, and leaving the task of reloading to his servant. In most cases, these simply were two guns, perhaps by the same maker or perhaps not, probably similar but not necessarily identical. You'll find some true pairs of flintlock or percussion guns, but relatively very few compared with the number of matched breechloaders, and by far the majority of those were built during or just after the late Victorian and Edwardian periods; during the time, in other words, when the English sporting gun was the symbol of an age.

Here, too, were practical reasons. The driven shoots were high volume affairs, several hundred birds brought to bag in a typical day by eight or ten shooters, and with the air literally full of wings, a man with only one gun found himself decidedly short on firepower, even with a stuffer standing by to drop in fresh cartridges after every two shots.

In the early 1880s, some sought to better their armament by ordering three-barrel guns from such makers as Edwinson Green of Cheltenham and Dickson's of Edinburgh. In London, Charles Lancaster built some four-barrel pieces and even imported a few Spencer pump guns from the United States. These oddments are the rare exceptions, though. Most Victorian shooters decided that the ideal solution was two guns combined with the services of a trained loader.

Usually they were identical twins, built at the same time by the same maker to the same specifications and cased together, as Macdonald Hastings puts it, "like a bridal couple," and accompanied by a trousseau of turn-screws, cleaning rods, striker pots, extra springs, gizmos, and gadgetry. In some ways, they represent gunmaking at its ultimate reach.

At this point, I believe a digression on terminology is in order. The language of multiple guns is sometimes confusing, because the British tend to use terms different from ours, or in some cases use the same terms to denote different things. Even then, consistency is not absolute, and there are a few words on which there seems to be no general agreement anywhere. But to be sure we're all reading off the same page, or at least from the same chapter, here's what I've learned from experience and from talking with people in the gun trade and related fields.

The most basic term is simply "pair," which to the British means two identical guns, built at the same time, with consecutive serial numbers and marked as No. 1 and No. 2. We commonly describe this as a "matched pair." The English sometimes do, too, but to them a matched pair usually is what we call a "composed pair," two identical guns built some time apart and therefore not bearing consecutive serial numbers. As a typical scenario, let's say a gentleman orders a single gun and three or four years later has a second built exactly like it; they may or may not be marked No. 1 and No. 2. The British would call these a matched pair, or occasionally, a composed pair; we'd call them a composed pair, but never a matched pair. Now, lest this should seem too simple, you'll sometimes hear "composed pair" used to describe similar but essentially unrelated guns that have somehow ended up together. I suspect this sort of pair more often than not begins as a double case and a single gun that just happens to fit inside it; find another single gun by the same maker that also fits, and you have a composed pair, at least of sorts.

Add one or more guns to the equation, and the terminology changes. For the most part, three or more identical guns are collectively called a "set." In a true set, as in a true pair, all were built at the same time, consecutively numbered, and marked Nos. 1, 2, 3 and so on. Composed sets are also possible. My friend Geoffrey Boothroyd, the dean of British gun writers, told me of a certain set of Dicksons that started as a pair, No. 1 and No. 2. No. 3 was added later and No. 4 built later still to match 1, 2, and 3, altogether a composed set of four.

I've also run across the words "garniture" and "leash" denoting a set of three, but these are not widely used. Sotheby's auction house uses garniture to describe three-item sets of porcelain and silver, but not guns. Geoffrey Boothroyd, on the other hand, says, "I have always felt 'garniture' meant guns one, two or three in a fitted case with all matching tools, a term taken from furniture, I think."

"Leash" originally referred to three hounds, a brace and a half of dogs, tied together on one leash. It eventually came to denote anything tied together in threes, and while it does sometimes refer to guns, it seems to be the least used of alternative terms.

So now we have that cleared up...assuming you haven't flung away your book and run shrieking to the liquor cabinet for a mind straightener.

Actually using a pair or set of guns is complicated in itself, although it's a snap compared with talking about them. Learning to pass guns back and forth without dropping them, bashing them together, or accidentally shooting someone takes a bit of practice, but anyone with enough coordination to blink and belch at the same time can soon get the hang of it. As for results, Lord Ripon summed it up nicely in 1911: "A quick shooter will fire his two guns and four barrels almost as if they were on one stock."

Ripon would have known, for he was by universal acclaim the finest shot in England throughout the years when shooting was at its peak. With his set of three Purdey hammer guns and two loaders, he could time and again have six pheasants dead in the air at once. On one occasion at Sandringham, the royal estate, he killed twenty-eight in a minute. (He liked to lend the impression that his brilliant skill came naturally, as he once wrote, "Quickness in letting off the second or even the third gun is no doubt to a great extent a matter of practice." But the wife of Lord Balfour noted in her journal that Ripon "was not too pleased at being discovered" in an estate house library practicing changing guns with his loaders in the middle of the night.)

As the great age of shooting blossomed, the gun trade continued to refine its products with an eye toward reaching the pinnacle of efficiency. Beginning with Joseph Needham's patent of 1874, ejectors of one design or another became standard fare, followed by self-opening actions and single triggers. Inevitably, a great many inventions and so-called improvements were frivolous or downright silly, but the truly important innovations like the Purdey bolt and the Scott spindle, nitro powders and various self-cocking hammerless actions brought the sporting gun to the point of perfection by the turn of the twentieth century.

Although the most famous shots of the day, the royal family, Lord Ripon, and Lord Walsingham, to name only a few, tended to buy their guns at Purdey's and Holland's, all of the best London makers enjoyed the vigorous custom of the times. And wherever he got them, anyone who ordered guns in pairs or sets paid a premium.

This is still true today. Every gun trade, whether in London, Birmingham, Eibar, St. Etienne, or the Val Trompia, charges more for pairs than for simply making two individual guns. The additional lug, which the London trade calls "pairing money," may run from five to twenty percent; part is kept by the company and part is passed along to the men who do the work.

To understand the extra charge, consider the factors that make a true pair something more than just two guns. First of all, everything about them must be as nearly identical as possible. This is simple enough for materials until you get to the wood. Every piece of wood, no matter what species the tree, is unique in grain structure, figure, and density. The more elaborate the figure, the more difficult it is to find two pieces that are even similar, much less a match. Truly matching stock blanks must be cut side by side from the same block, and you can sort through a hell of a lot of lumber to find a block that will yield two blanks two inches thick, both with exactly the right grain structure for gunstocks, aesthetically pleasing figure, and no major flaws in either one.

The monetary rule of thumb for these is "two for the price of three," two truly matching chunks of wood for the same price as three of equal quality that don't match. In England at the moment, matching blanks of best-quality French walnut sell for about £3000 per pair or roughly $5000, depending upon exchange rates.

On appearance alone, matching stocks probably do more to define a pair of guns than any other element. Or as one of my gunning partners puts it, quoting a phrase from the Lutheran hymnal, a true pair are sisters in the wood.

But of course there's more to it, quite a lot more, in fact. A true pair aren't just look-alikes. They are the same in every detail, from trigger pulls to ejector timing to a finished weight that shouldn't vary a fraction of an ounce from one to the other. Creating this demands craftsmanship of the highest level, and that's where the price premium really goes.

In their turn, the craftsmen sometimes refer to pairing money as "PITA money," an acronym of which the first letter stands for "pain." And it's painstaking work. The only way to build two or more truly identical guns is to build them simultaneously, not one after the other, and they're built that way from beginning to end. The barrelmaker starts with four tubes. Switching from one to the other at every step, he makes two sets of barrels at the same time, identical to the thousandth parts of inches and ounces. The action filer does the same with two forgings.

So does the stockmaker; when one blank is headed up, he heads up the other, fits one trigger plate and then the second, hangs one set of triggers and then the other, shapes one and then the other, step by step, checking both against the same gauges. In the end, they will be exactly the same in every external dimension, not just the gross dimensions of pull and bend and cast, but in every way, from the diameter of the hand to the length of the thumb hole to the radius of the butt.

Because the two blanks may differ slightly in density, balancing can be a special problem. The stocker may have to bore four ounces out of one and only an ounce out of the other in order that both guns weigh the same and balance at precisely the same point. Then he has to checker them with not one line or diamond's difference between the two.

The engraver eventually will do the same thing, creating duplicate designs and patterns that should be no more different than images in a mirror. Or at least he did years ago. Nowadays, when game scenes and portraiture are popular decoration, pairs often feature different birds or dogs.

If it's all done properly, the only way anyone should be able to tell which gun is which is to look at the serial number or the gun number, inlaid in gold or simply engraved on the top lever, on the rib at the breech, and on the forend tip. And then, for a shooter whose technique is consistent, they will truly fit Lord Ripon's image of four barrels on a single stock.

Although the terrible carnage of World War I and the economic hardships of its aftermath brought the great age of shooting to a close, the best part of its spirit has never died. Driven shooting no longer involves seven-course dinners and costume balls, but such frippery is no great loss. The quality of the sport and sportsmanship is still there, in England and on the Continent as well, and so are the opportunities for shooting a pair of guns.

In fact, such opportunities are more widely available now than they ever were in Prince Edward's time. Political changes have opened doors to shooting in eastern Europe that were closed for most of the century, and only now are the riches of South American game growing fully appreciated. The shooting in Argentina and Uruguay and Colombia hasn't anything like the formalities of Old World sport, but no matter. One chap I know does his South American dove shooting with a lovely pair of Spanish sidelocks, spends a half hour at the beginning of each trip showing his bird boy the trick of changing guns, and has a whale of a good time.

Even if you never use them both at once, a pair of guns has a special appeal to anyone who appreciates tradition and the sort of craftsmanship that serves to define what best quality really is. Perhaps that's why people still order new pairs built and why we covet the old ones. There's something about them that adds up to more than just the sum of two guns.

Part of it lies simply in finding a pair that's managed to stay together all these years. As the fortunes of the British upper class declined in the 1920s and '30s, a great many pairs and sets of guns were sold off and ultimately broken up, separated from their mates. You can find them now by the dozen, single guns whose numbers show that somewhere in the world are others just like them.

One English company, Matched Pairs Ltd., specializes in bringing pairs and sets back together, but it's seldom an easy task and not always economical. A gun dealer friend of mine in Somerset once told me that reuniting pairs is the bane of his existence. "Even if I'm lucky enough to find the bloody things, it usually comes down to a stand-off," he said. "Each owner wants to buy the other gun, nobody wants to sell, and I end up without a shilling for my trouble."

Being a freelancer myself, I can sympathize with Jonathan's plight, but on the other hand, I also understand how the desire to buy can hold the upper hand. My own favorite fowling piece is the No. 1 gun of a pair built in 1916. Where the other one is I haven't a clue, and that's probably just as well. So long as it's out there in the unknown I don't have to deal with the problem of how to afford it, nor do I have to tell some kindred soul that I'm unwilling to satisfy his dream by selling mine.

But I hope he gets the same feeling from his that mine gives me, the same sense that here, in this lovely old gun, is the image of a world that can never come again but is at the same time a world that will never completely disappear.

3

A CENTURY OF
GUNS

Call the twentieth century the Space Age, the Age of Information, or what you will, but talk of guns and, damn, it was a time.

It was shaped by the rifle, from the 1914–1918 affair that was supposed to be the be-all and end-all of war, to the even more destructive one that lasted from 1939 to 1945, to the subsequent thermonuclear tensions that threatened to be the end-all of everything. Toss in a couple of dustups in Korea and Viet Nam, and it was, by anyone's definition, a century defined by firepower.

For the shotgun, it was both the best and the worst of times. It ended much as it began—and did so to nearly everyone's surprise.

The classic game gun, as defined by the British, was perfect before the twentieth century began. By 1900, the breechloader was as highly evolved as it will ever be, an elegant, graceful instrument combining beauty and useful-ness to an extent that no item of human manufacture will ever surpass. All its refinements were well in place. Rebounding locks, hammerless locks, safety sears, ejectors, choke boring, self-opening actions, single triggers—everything that is "modern" about the classic side-by-side gun is more than a hundred years old.

Even the over/under took shape early on, its future charted by Boss in 1909, by Woodward in 1912, and by Browning in 1926.

So, the double gun met the twentieth century in full flower, but the full flower of the twentieth century was not long in meeting the double gun. Our infatuation with the machine was nothing new in 1900, but its application to guns was only just beginning. John Browning invented both the Winchester Model 1897 pump gun and the Browning Auto-5, first manufactured in 1902; both were seminal to the guns the twentieth century would embrace.

World War I, till then the most highly mechanized war in history, was the first turning point, sweeping away in one brief cataclysm the old, graceful age in which the double gun had flourished. Tradition struggled to maintain its balance, but in England and Europe, virtually an entire generation of future craftsmen were gone.

In the United States, hand craftsmanship was already on the wane, subsumed by the economics of machine manufacture. World War I brought a truly great age of American gunmaking virtually to a close. With few exceptions, the finest of all Parkers, Foxes, L.C. Smiths, and others were built before we became actively involved in the European conflict. They show a level of fit and finish and sheer attention to detail that most later guns do not.

The passing of the Golden Age became even more apparent in the late 1920s. The overall quality of American guns was noticeably diminished even before the stock market crash of 1929. Manufacturing costs climbed steadily as the gun market's purchasing power declined or was diluted by a growing interest in repeaters.

That the double gun survived the 1930s at all is a wonder. The Great Depression shook the entire world. Literally dozens of once-great English makers struggled, amalgamated, or closed down altogether. As only one example of a phenomenon widespread in the English trade, Stephen Grant & Sons purchased Joseph Lang & Son in 1925; by 1939, the amalgamation included Harrison & Hussey, Charles Lancaster, Watson Bros., and Frederick Beesley. By 1976, Henry Atkin, Charles Hellis, E.J. Churchill, and Webley

& Scott were part of the group as well. In all, ten gunmakers that once were viable, independent businesses ended up huddled together in a desperate attempt at survival.

World War II was the last nail in an already virtually airtight coffin. The sheer destruction of it extinguished the market for sporting guns across most of Europe and Asia; the terrible toll of human life erased much of yet another generation of gunmaking craftsmen; and the awesome capacity for firepower spawned by the war left the remaining market utterly devoted to repeating guns. When American GIs returned home to resume their lives as hunters, they had no interest in two-shot guns. They wanted pumps and, especially, autoloaders—both of which the arms industry was well prepared to provide at very low cost. Firepower had won the war, and it won the subsequent peace as well.

By 1950, all but one of the great American double guns were gone, and not even the Winchester Model 21 would have survived had John Olin not insisted that it remain in production regardless of its inability to generate a profit.

The situation in Europe was little better. Only a handful of English makers remained, struggling desperately to stay afloat. Had they known at the time that their plight would continue for more than thirty years, I suspect they all would have thrown in the towel.

Mercifully, they didn't. They hung on as best they could while the gun market continued to pass them by. Who, after all, wanted a double gun?

Some of us did. At first, in the 1960s, we represented no great numbers, a trickle here and there, just some guys who felt inexplicably drawn to the traditions of our grandfathers in ways that our fathers' pump guns and autoloaders couldn't quite satisfy. By the 70s it was clear that the quantity of game we knew in the 50s was disappearing under the machinery and chemicals of modern agriculture, and firepower began to lose its lustre in an awakening sense of quality experience.

Not, of course, that the gun solely defines the quality of a hunt, nor that two or three or a half-dozen birds are any more meaningful shot with a double than with a pump when the man behind the gun owns a genuine love for grouse or pheasants, quail or ducks. But when numbers are no longer the guiding principle we tend to take a broader view of quality, and what's more appropriate to a beautiful bird than a truly beautiful gun?

19

The double gun's momentum began to regather in the mid-1980s, from trickles to streams. Order books in London gradually swelled. Gunmakers in Italy and Spain who'd played for years to local audiences found themselves entering the spotlight of international recognition. Tom Skeuse's Parker Reproduction proved that the technology that once spelled the demise of the American double could now be the instrument of its resurrection.

Even so, none of us was really prepared for what the 1990s would bring. Who'da thunk that the last year of the century would once again see the double gun reign supreme, or that the gun world would be more vibrant than it's been at any time since World War I?

It was by any definition a remarkable decade. In 1989, only about a dozen English gunmakers remained in business, several of whom were surviving on repair work alone. Now there are more than two dozen, all turning out new guns, some on a very limited basis but others booked up with orders that will take three or four years to fill. In 1989, fewer than a handful of top-quality Italian makers were widely known outside Europe, or even outside Italy; now, if you want to place an order with Fratelli Rizzini, Piotti, Fabbri, Bosis, Ferlib, Bertuzzi, or any of a dozen others, you'll have to take a place in line.

If you'd mentioned Spanish guns to an American shooter ten years ago you'd have been greeted with sneering comments about the cheap, crudely built boxlocks that earned such an awful reputation here in the 60s and 70s. Mention them now and you'll hear nothing but fond praise for the sidelock Arrietas, AyAs, Garbis, Grullas, Ugartecheas, and Arrizabalagas that represent the best values available anywhere in the world. The guns were there all along, but it wasn't till the 1990s that they finally gained the recognition they deserve.

And American guns—oh, my. The Parker Reproduction was the first step, of course, a fine demonstration of what cutting-edge technology could do by way of cloning an American classic. But the notion of actually manufacturing high-quality double guns in this country seemed out of the question even when the Parker Repro was in its heyday. Even so, A.H. Fox and the Winchester Model 21 are back in production, both built entirely in the United States; the grand old Ithaca NID came back, too, built partly in Italy and partly here—which is also true of the new Dakota Arms side-by-side; and Lefevers probably will be with us again as well in a few years. In the magnificent A. Galazan sidelock over/under, made wholly in the U.S. by Connecticut Shotgun Manufacturing Company, we have what is unquestionably the finest gun ever built in America, a gun made to levels of quality equal to anything you can get from Italy or England. And it all happened in the 90s.

In 1999 alone, the venerable firm of Auguste Francotte found a new lease on life through a merger with the brilliant Dutch maker Tom Derksen, and the two most famous Scottish names of all time—Dickson and MacNaughton—were reorganized and financed to become active gunmakers once again.

What caused all this? There's no question that a thriving global economy contributed the environment, but an environment is only a means wherein a phenomenon can take place. If disposable income alone were the key, the double-gun renaissance should have happened in the 50s. The real cause, I believe, lies closer to the working of the human spirit. Technology, especially electronics, opened a whole new world in 1945, and we went on a forty-year orgy of exploring its possibilities, created and embraced every application, no matter how frivolous, from the transistor radio to MTV to video games. Only when it was almost too late did we realize that the real value of technology might lie in preserving what once was the product of our hands guided by our hearts.

George Santayana speculated that those who fail to understand history are doomed to repeat it. This is true, but it's also true that those who fail to appreciate history are doomed to lose it—and thereby lose not only our best achievements but, even worse, lose sight of why we set out to accomplish them in the first place. The renascence of the double gun has something to do with a widespread ability to pay the price but more to do with a widespread recognition of its value.

The Parker Reproduction proved beyond question that computer-driven machinery can replicate the body, if not quite the soul, of a fine gun at a reasonable price. The guns built now, from Italy to England to the U.S., prove that machine applications combined with traditional hand-work can capture everything a fine gun was ever meant to be. That these nineteenth-century items exist at all in the dawn of the twenty-first century is one thing; that the gun world is truly thriving is quite another. However else we may choose to remember the twentieth century, those of us who love the gun can only wonder and be thankful that history does move in circles, after all.

4

LIKE A SPANIEL
WITHOUT EARS

Time was, a gun with two barrels was thought quaintly old-fashioned. A generation steeped in the sheer firepower so well demonstrated in World War II wondered why anyone would want a gun that shot only twice when he could have one that held anywhere from three to seven cartridges at a single loading.

That same generation looked upon a two-barreled gun with exposed hammers as hopelessly obsolete—a grandfather gun, even at a time when Grandad himself most likely shot a Winchester or Remington pump or a Browning A-5. A gun with hammers—"ear hammers" they were often called, or "mule ears"—was an artifact positively prehistoric in comparison to the mechanical systems available at prices nearly anyone could afford.

Consequently, virtually every gunshop with even a modest inventory sported a few old hammer guns, quietly gathering dust and seldom earning a second glance.

And in fact, a lot of them hardly deserved even a first glance. From about 1880 till the beginning of World War I, the American market was awash with hammer, and hammerless, guns cheaply built in Belgium or by such stateside factories as Crescent Fire Arms in Connecticut. These so-called "contract guns" were sold as house brands by scores of hardware and sporting-goods dealers under the names of gun companies that never existed except on paper. No one knows exactly how many of these brand names there were; current count is well over 200.

Because they were cheaply made and cheaply sold, a great many had fallen to pieces by the 1950s and 60s. And because a lot of them had twist or Damascus barrels, the survivors were shunned as disasters waiting to happen if combined with current, nitro-powder cartridges. Some were disasters, and some happened. Even those barreled in so-called "fluid" steel weren't really very durable; if the barrels didn't blow out, actions were almost certain to shoot loose.

The equations were simple. Hammer gun = antique. Hammer gun with twist barrels = dangerous antique. So, such guns were pointedly ignored except by a few chaps who found them interesting, if rather funky, reminders of a bygone age. Collecting contract guns was, moreover, an inexpensive pastime. Ten or 15 dollars would buy almost any of them, and if you paid as much as $30 you were probably getting skinned.

Truly high-quality English and Belgian hammer guns sometimes surfaced in the sea of junk, but few possessed the knowledge to recognize them—and the warnings against Damascus barrels had by then become so ingrained that nobody was willing to pay much for an unshootable gun.

Times change. So do tastes. Interest in double guns began to perk around 1980 and steadily gathered momentum among collectors and shooters alike. With game-bird populations declining in many parts of the country, hunters rediscovered the double's wonderful handling qualities and reckoned that if bag limits were growing smaller, taking those few birds with a lovely old gun added an element to the sport that wasn't available from a repeater, even if it could hold half a box of shells. In short, American hunters more interested in experience than in simply gathering meat recognized the double gun as a direct link to the best traditions of the sport.

Take those traditions a step farther back in time, and rediscovery of hammer guns became inevitable. This began in the early 1990s, and over the ensuing decade, the alchemy of romance transformed hammer guns from dross to gold.

As shooters became more sophisticated with regard to their guns, more and more of them learned how to recognize the difference between grain and chaff. Nowadays, interest in hammer guns is greater than at any time in living memory. Call it regression on a 150-year scale, but it bears an element of soul not easily described.

Aesthetics certainly are a part. To my eye, there is no gun so elegant as a top-quality hammer piece. Because I know something of what went into its creation, a fine hammer gun strikes me as the ultimate reach of hand craftsmanship. Some workman stood at his bench for hours, days, patiently filing hammers in the mirror image of one another, sculpting fences in graceful curves and planes, filing triggers to a form as slender as a lady's ankle. Combine such skills with those of a master barrelmaker, a first-rate stocker, and the decorative touches of a skillful engraver, and you have something that transcends time in the same manner as a piece of fine art.

I spent years looking for just the right hammer gun until it ultimately found me—a vintage-1886 Purdey 12-bore with isolated, back-action locks set into a stock that shows considerably more figure than was customary at the time. The sheer grace of its lines and its consummate craftsmanship are a continual source of delight. I suspect that anyone who knew how much time I spend just turning it over and over in my hands in simple admiration would think me rather simple. And perhaps rightly so. I love all my game guns for how they look and feel and perform, but there's something about that old Purdey that draws me as inexorably as I am drawn to my wife, and for many of the same reasons—breathtaking to behold, irresistible in substance.

It was originally barreled in solid steel, sleeved with new steel tubes in 1988 and reproofed in London. Of all the parts to a hammer gun—or any old gun, for that matter—barrels require the most knowledge and the most sensible caution. Right now, the demand for English hammer guns is such that dealers are literally combing British country pubs and buying wallhangers to resell in the United States. Some are good, some aren't, and the crucial elements begin with barrels.

Comparing the thinking of the 1950s with the thinking in some quarters now, the pendulum seems to have swung to its full extent. We've gone from All Damascus is Bad to All Damascus is Good. Neither is the case.

Some Damascus barrels are perfectly good for reasonable modern ammunition; some others, no matter how pristine they appear, truly are the old disasters waiting to happen. The original level of proof is one key, current condition is quite another.

A lot of old Damascus barrels were proofed with black powder only. That doesn't in itself mean they're unsafe with nitro cartridges. Some others were originally nitro-proofed, but similarly, that doesn't mean they're safe to shoot now.

Some old black-powder barrels will stand current proof perfectly well, and some old nitro-proofed barrels won't. Don't be mislead by a nitro-proof mark that's a hundred-odd years old—simply because you don't know what's been done to the barrels in the meantime. They may have been rebored, restruck, or otherwise modified in ways that render original proof invalid.

Take this as the rule of thumb: Do not consider any twist or Damascus barrels safe unless they've recently been reproofed for modern ammunition by one of the British or European proof houses. This applies to every gun of any origin, and particularly to American guns. Proof laws have been in force in Britain and European countries for 400 years or more. The United States has never had a uniform code of firearms proof; it's always been up to individual makers to conduct proof tests on their own. American makers bought most of their Damascus tubes from Belgium or England. These were usually top-quality in original form, but you have no way of knowing how far from original form they are now.

Damascus barrels can ring like bells and shine like new dimes inside and out. A good ring means only that the ribs are still well secured. Shine can mean anything from pristine original condition to repolishing that may have left the walls thin as paper. Superficial examination and even careful measuring cannot reveal the condition of the occlusions between the skelps of iron and steel that constitute Damascus or twist. And trust me, there is no so-called "expert" who can realistically vet barrels just by looking. The real expert will tell you that reproof is the only reliable test.

Having a set of barrels reproofed by an English or other European proof house is neither difficult nor particularly expensive—dirt-cheap, actually, when you consider that not having it done may cost you anything from a couple of fingers to an entire leading hand, and a wrecked gun besides.

With barrels, you just have to harden your heart. Forget about how beautiful the gun may be, and forget about what any dealer or barrel man might tell you about the condition of any set of tubes. If there is no recent reproof mark in evidence, there is no evidence on which to suppose that those barrels are safe.

Besides demanding some hard-nosed insistence upon the condition of barrels, hammer guns require rethinking in how they are to be handled. All modern guns have safety mechanisms, including some currently made hammer guns. The old ones generally do not. For those, "safe" is either rebounding locks or a half-cock notch on the tumbler. As we are now at least three generations removed from familiarity with hammer guns in general, safe handling is a particular issue.

You have some choices. One is to leave the hammers at rebound or half-cock position and cock them both when you're ready to shoot. This requires a strong trigger hand and a fairly long thumb, one that can lever both hammer spurs at the same time. If you're physically capable, this is a good means for shooting doves, ducks, or driven game.

Another, perhaps even safer, approach is to cock both hammers and crack the action slightly open for carrying. Open action means that an accidental pull on a trigger will be harmless because the striker cannot reach the cartridge primer. This, too, is good for doves, ducks, and driven birds.

For other upland shooting—quail, pheasants, grouse, or other birds likely to spring up without notice—neither of these options is ideal. Trying to cock hammers or close an action when birds are in the air is at best a comedy of errors that's apt to leave you howling like a ruptured panther and your companions rolling on the ground, laughing their heads off. I've tried carrying hammer guns every way there is and found only one that's truly efficient.

This simply is to cock both hammers and carry the gun with muzzles up, my thumb between the hammers for a secure hold, and one or two fingers over the guard to stave off brush or anything else that might snag a trigger. As my gun weighs only 6¼ pounds, it's comfortable to carry that way—and perfectly safe so long as the muzzles are pointing harmlessly upward. In places where the footing is such that I might stumble and fall, I simply uncock the gun before wading through.

I wish it had a tang safety, partly because clicking a thumb-piece is for me an unconscious element in swinging and mounting a gun, and partly because a mechanical safety is yet one more layer of protection against firing an accidental shot.

But relying upon any mechanical system to the extent of ignoring the muzzles is a ticket to catastrophe. Control of the muzzles is control of safety.

In some ways, a hammer gun is safer than a hammerless. You can tell at a glance whether a hammer gun is cocked; with a hammerless gun, you have to assume that it's cocked any time the action is closed. And you can readily uncock a hammer gun without unloading it. Depending upon how the fastener is designed, you can uncock some hammer guns just by opening the action and easing the hammers down with your thumb. With others— and my Purdey is one—the right hammer has to be let down with the action closed. To do so, I turn away from my companions and dogs, point the muzzles at the ground and thumb the right hammer down. Should it slip because of an insecure grasp or cold hands or whatever, the shot goes harmlessly into the dirt. With the right hammer down, I can open the action to uncock the left one with no possible harm at all.

Some Italian makers—notably Abbiatico & Salvinelli, Fratelli Bertuzzi, and Fratelli Piotti—have built self-cocking hammer guns fitted with tang safeties. The self-cocking part is not a new concept. In the 1870s, Thomas Perkes patented a system that involves a T-shaped arm fitted into a gun's standing breech; rotating the top lever lifts the arm, which contacts the necks of the hammers and pushes them to full cock. A number of London makers adopted this mechanism during the transitional period between hammer and hammerless actions. Later systems, including those currently used in Italy, are based on the Holland & Holland-style system of cocking by internal levers—no different, really, from the way most hammerless doubles are cocked today.

In staid and steadfast Britain, hammer guns remained the favorites of some long after the hammerless breechloader became standard. Lord Ripon, acclaimed as the finest game shot in England from the 1870s till he went face-down in the heather of a grouse moor in 1923, shot a trio of Purdey hammer guns through a career that accounted for better than a quarter-million birds. Except for being best-quality ejector models, Ripon's guns looked just like mine. I wish I could say I shoot mine as well as he shot his.

But there was that day in South Dakota last season when I was a blocker and a big, gaudy rooster flew the gauntlet of walkers and was still cackling invective when he came barreling past me about thirty yards out. A Toyota's-length of forward allowance, a touch to the back trigger, and he went head-first into the corn stubble. If a gun could purr, I imagine mind did right then.

King George V, another inveterate hammer-gun man, once remarked that "a gun without hammers is like a spaniel without ears." None of my spaniels have heard that without giving me a baleful glare, so I don't figure to test the truth of it. But so long as I can caress a puppy's ears with one hand and a pair of beautifully filed hammers with the other, I'll go on assuming that His Majesty was right.

5

THE HONOR
ROLL

Ever wonder how your gun got to be
the way it is? Why its mechanics work one way rather than another? Whose
idea was what, and when?

The history of the gun is a chronicle of evolution. By the same token,
it also is a history studded with endpoints—mechanical systems brought to
such a level of perfection that they subsequently became the standards of
their kind, and became in turn the milestones of their particular evolutionary branches.

Many such things mark the development of the gun; the flintlock, the
caplock, certainly the breechloader and the self-contained cartridge all qualify as inventions that helped shape evolution. So does Henry Nock's patent
breech, invented in 1787; it was arguably the single most important step in
the perfection of the muzzle-loading gun.

But the muzzle-loader was, of course, only a stage in the evolution of
the modern gun. The Frenchman Casimir Lefaucheaux didn't invent the

breechloader—German gunmakers were building breechloading flintlocks as early as the sixteenth century—but Lefaucheaux's break-action pinfire gun, displayed in London at the Great Exhibition of 1851, was the version that caught everyone's interest. Similarly, another Frenchman, named Pottet, didn't invent the self-contained cartridge, either, but his became the model upon which the modern cartridge is based.

From a twenty-first-century perspective, the modern gun is a hammerless affair with barrels arranged either side by side or one atop the other. And you could argue that the ultramodern gun has only one barrel, supplied from a magazine and operated either by a slide-handle or by mechanisms that cause it to reload itself without any effort on the shooter's part. They're all equally valid evolutionary branches, and all have their salient endpoints. To discuss every one would fill a hefty book, or several, but in each branch there are some highlights that strike me as shining a bit brighter than the rest. Call it the honor roll, the summa cum laude of mechanical achievement that has helped create perfection in the guns we use today.

Chronologically, we can start in 1863, when James Purdey the Younger received a patent for the double-bite underbolt fastener.

In the early days of the break-action breechloader, the main problem wasn't how to make a gun open but rather how to keep it closed. If a gun is to function efficiently, and safely, it has to have a close, tight fit between barrels and breech. Whatever mechanism is used to accomplish this must, moreover, be durable enough to withstand both the wear endemic to moving parts and the stresses exerted by burning gunpowder. Lefaucheaux's original approach, using a single, sliding underbolt that engages a notch in the barrel lump, was a good concept but given the state of metallurgy at the time, not particularly durable.

Ultimately, gunmakers tried just about everything—bolts, cross-pins, screw grips, breech covers, you name it—but the most elegant solution for the side-by-side gun was Purdey's bolt. It moves horizontally in the frame, and its two bearing surfaces and corresponding twin bites in the barrel lump proved fully capable of fastening the action of even the largest big-bore rifles. Combined with an equally simple and efficient top-lever spindle invented by William Scott of Birmingham in 1865, the Purdey bolt has ever after been the standard in the European trade.

The next important step came in 1875, with the first hammerless action that cocked itself. A gun with exposed hammers is simple to cock; pull 'em back with your thumb, and you're ready to go. Hammers concealed inside the frame are another story, and at first, gunmakers used some form of lever to cock the locks. In some cases, it was the same lever that opened the action, in others, a separate system. Lever-cocking worked, but gunmakers of the time knew there had to be a more efficient approach.

William Anson and John Deeley, working for Westley Richards & Co. of Birmingham, were the first to find it. In their design, patented in 1875, the lockwork is cocked by leverage from the barrels. The Anson & Deeley system is the soul of simplicity, comprising only three basic lock parts: a tumbler or hammer, a main spring, and a sear. The hammer is shaped with a long toe that reaches forward in the action bar and engages one end of a cocking lever. The other end of the lever protrudes through the action knuckle and fits into a notch in the forend iron. As the barrels pivot on the hinge pin, the forend iron moves the cocking lever, which in turn lifts the hammer until the sear engages.

Besides the cocking concept, which in one form or another is the world-standard approach, the Anson & Deeley action is also notable in that it was the first example of what we now know as the boxlock gun—a form in which the lock parts are fastened to the gun's frame rather than mounted on removable sideplates. Not all subsequent boxlocks are true Anson & Deeley type, strictly speaking, but the Anson & Deeley is where they all began.

The same cocking system works equally well for sidelock guns, and what now is the world-standard sidelock action was developed in the 1880s and '90s by Henry Holland, as the Holland & Holland Royal Model side-by-side. It, too, is brilliantly simple, wonderfully efficient. Some makers, notably Beesley and Boss, invented their own proprietary actions, but once the patents expired, virtually the entire gunmaking world adopted the Holland action. With only a few exceptions, the sidelock side-by-side guns built today in England, France, Spain, Italy, and elsewhere are made in the Holland & Holland image.

Ejectors and single triggers are the most significant refinements to the modern gun, and the most important versions of both were perfected around 1893.

Of the literally hundreds of ejector systems invented in the past hundred-odd years, the one most widely copied today is known as the Southgate—even though its namesake, London gunmaker Thomas Southgate, neither invented the concept nor refined it to its simplest form. The classic Southgate ejector comprises only a cam-shaped tumbler and a spring, and it operates on the over-center principle. When the point of the cam is at a precise right angle to the upper limb of the spring, the tumbler is at equilibrium. But when the tumbler is rotated, it goes past equilibrium—over-center, in other words—and the spring spins it sharply, driving the striking surface against the ejector stem. This is the same principle that keeps a pocketknife open or closed, depending on which way you rotate the blade.

The Southgate system was originally developed for the side-by-side gun, but it eventually was adapted to the over/under as well. And while it is by no means the only system in use today, it is, as I said, the most widely copied worldwide.

Firing two barrels with only one trigger proved a more difficult problem to solve. A number of English gunmakers came up with single-trigger mechanisms in the 1880s, but nobody figured out how to make one that didn't fire both barrels at once till about 1892, when John Robertson and William Adams started experimenting with the mechanics.

Robertson, himself a practical gunmaker, owned the old firm of Boss & Company; Adams was a Boss craftsman. Together, they discovered that the double discharges that plagued single triggers were not the result of the first shot jarring off the second sear, as everyone assumed, but instead happened because shooters pull the trigger twice on every shot.

Here's what happens: As we fire a shot, the gun recoils backward and as it does, we release the trigger. But then we unconsciously push the gun forward in response to the recoil; this brings our finger back in contact with the trigger, and we pull it again, without ever realizing that we've done it. It's known as the "involuntary pull," and we all do it, every time.

Once they understood the real nature of the problem, Robertson and Adams had little difficulty in devising a mechanism to solve it, and with the final patent, issued in November 1894, they created the first truly successful single trigger for a double gun. Many others have since invented equally reliable systems that work on differing principles of physics and mechanics, but every single trigger that exists today incorporates some means of accommodating the involuntary pull. Some use the unconscious pull to shift from one sear to the other, others render it harmless by either blocking or disconnecting the trigger from the sears, but they're all designed in the knowledge that we pull the trigger twice for every shot we fire.

Boss & Company achieved another landmark in 1909, with the introduction of its over/under gun. It certainly wasn't the first over/under built either in England or in Europe; German craftsmen were making stack-barrels as far back as the flintlock era. The Boss, however, was the over/under that represented the first step on the path toward the future.

Neither the barrel lump and cross-pin hinge nor the sliding underbolt fastener that are so perfectly suited to the side-by-side are optimal for an over/under. They work mechanically, of course; for proof of that you need look no further than the venerable Browning Superposed. But placing barrels one on top of the other creates a tall profile to begin with, and hanging a lump underneath the bottom one only makes it taller still. This in turn means that the frame has to be proportionately deeper, which adds additional weight to the gun and does nothing in aid of an already-awkward appearance.

By contrast, the Boss is about as elegantly slender and light as an over/under can be, and this is the result of two things: a trunnion-type hinge and a fastening system that engages at mid-breech rather than underneath.

The gun was largely the invention of Boss actioner Bob Henderson, and it has those cardinal virtues of a truly great over/under: a slender, relatively slim frame that promotes not only dynamic balance but also splendid pointing qualities as well.

For the hinge, Henderson borrowed a concept from canonry. Strictly speaking, a trunnion is an integral protrusion on either side of a cannon, meant to support the barrel in some sort of base, cradle, or caisson. In the early days, when a cannon was literally nothing more than a barrel, trunnions not only provided a means of support, but also a means of adjusting elevation.

Henderson clearly understood that you can apply the same concept to an over/under gun by putting rounded studs on either side of the bottom barrel and filing corresponding notches in the sides of the frame to form a hinge. He also understood that fastening bites in the middle of an over/under breech are every bit as effective as those in a barrel lump, possibly even stronger.

Since then, makers have devised all sorts of variations on these two concepts. Some use a reverse-trunnion hinge in which the studs are part of the frame rather than the barrels, and mid-breech fasteners run the gamut from tapered pins to sliding bolts. The principles, however, are the same. During the past forty years, the Italian gun trade has adopted the over/under as a signature form and has done with it what the English trade did with the side-by-side in the late nineteenth century, which is to say they've brought the over/under to perfection. If you look at the best of them—Fabbri, Perazzi, Beretta, Marocchi, Bosis, Bertuzzi, Abbiatico & Salvinelli, and others—you'll see trunnion hinges and mid-breech fasteners. If you look at the Boss over/under, you'll see where it all came from.

That all the inventions I've mentioned so far are English has less to do with Anglophilia than with the simple fact that the English perfected the side-by-side gun during the latter nineteenth century and created the role model for the over/under in the early twentieth century.

The American industry has built side-by-sides and over/unders, too. And we've made some good ones, though in my opinion only the A.H. Fox combines mechanical simplicity and elegant aesthetics on a level to match the English side-by-side. The old Remington Model 32 is one of the world's great over/unders, and so is the venerable Browning Superposed, certainly an American design though never actually made here. The magnificent A. Galazan sidelock over/under, currently built by Connecticut Shotgun Manufacturing Company, is as good as any made anywhere in the world.

Even so, the most historically important American contributions to the modern gun lie elsewhere. The first, and arguably the greatest of all, is the pump-action repeater.

Both English and French gunmakers patented early designs for slide actions, but only American makers actually built them. The Spencer, patented in April 1882, was the first successful pump; Winchester's Model 1897 was the first truly great one. You could argue that the Winchester Model 12 is the greatest of all, and I wouldn't disagree—except to say that Remington's Model 31 and Model 870 deserve full shares of the limelight as well. The Ithaca Model 37, which started as the Remington Model 17, is no slouch, either.

But all of them—in fact, all the pump guns of the twentieth century—owe much to the Winchester Model 97 and to the genius of John Browning, who literally created the modern age of repeating arms.

Winchester's first pump shotgun was the Model 1893, though it was the fifth slide action that Browning patented. It was a good gun, but it had a serious flaw.

Every repeater has to have some mechanism that allows the shooter to open the action, with or without a shot being fired. For the Model 93, Browning used one system to do both, actuated by the firing pin. To open the gun without firing it, you must either cock the hammer and push the firing pin forward with your finger, or else gently lower the hammer onto the pin. This obviously compromises safety, because if the hammer slips, the gun will go off.

More important, though, linking the breechbolt fastener to the firing pin means the action unlocks at the moment of firing. A shooter who's quick with the slide can have the action partway open while there's still some gas pressure in the barrel, and if there's any delay in ignition, he can have it partly, or even fully, open before the gun discharges. And that, to put it mildly, was not good, particularly as hang-fires weren't uncommon in those days and aren't unheard-of even now.

In September 1894, when production stood at about serial number 13000, Winchester engineers added a recoil lock and a slide-handle stop. That presumably helped mitigate the problem, but certainly didn't solve it. John Browning himself solved it, however, with a revised design that Winchester introduced in November 1897. And it was a solution that amounts to one of the most elegantly brilliant strokes of engineering ever applied to firearms.

Years ago, English engineer and gun writer G.T. Garwood, who wrote as "Gough Thomas," coined the word "eumatic" to denote the degree of compatibility between a tool and the human body. A single trigger that accommodates the shooter's involuntary pull is an example of perfect eumatics—and so is the action disconnector of the Model 97 Winchester, perfect in fact to the extent that the same principle has been used in every pump gun manufactured since.

To open a modern pump when it's cocked, you push a button located somewhere near the trigger guard, and the action unlocks without compromising safety at all. You also manually unlock the action after firing the gun—but what's so exquisitely elegant about Browning's system is that you do it unconsciously.

To unlock a pump gun after you've fired it, you have to push the slide-handle forward, which is exactly what we do in response to recoil. It's such a natural reaction that you can shoot pumps for a lifetime and never realize how they work.

If you want to test it, put a snap cap in your gun, pull the trigger without touching the slide-handle, and then try to open the action by pulling it back. Can't do it. Then push forward; with most guns, you can hear as well as feel the locking system disconnect. It's one of the simplest examples of pure genius I can think of.

The autoloader is another uniquely American form, and it, too, was originally the work of John Browning. In eumatic terms, I don't think it's quite as highly refined as the pump gun. An autoloader is solely at the mercy of its ammunition, and it will cycle only as fast as its mechanism allows. A pump, on the other hand, is only as slow as the guy working the slide. Not even the quickest shooter can speed up an autoloader's measured bang..bang..bang, but a really fast shot can make a pump gun sound like a chainsaw.

Nevertheless, there's no question that the self-loader is in some ways the ultimate repeater, nor that Browning's venerable A-5 squareback gun, described in a series of patents first issued in October 1900, affected the shooting world like the movement of tectonic plates.

Browning used recoil energy to make his autoloader work, and so did everyone else for the next fifty years. Some systems were decidedly better than others, but they were all based on recoil. The next milestone came when someone decided to use gas energy instead.

That, too, was a John Browning concept. Noticing that enough gas blew out the muzzle of a rifle barrel to scatter leaves and flatten grass, he tinkered up a system in 1890 that turned one of his Winchester lever-action rifles into a gas-operated autoloader that would fire a full sixteen-shot magazine in a minute or less. He subsequently developed the idea for pistols and machine guns, but never for a shotgun.

Nor did anyone else until Remington engineers started fooling with the notion in the mid-1950s. The Remington Model 58, introduced in 1956, was the first successful gas-operated gun, but the one that opened the way to the future was the Model 1100, invented by Wayne Leek and a team of Remington designers and put onto the market in 1963.

Essentially, the system works by diverting a portion of the gas generated by burning gunpowder and using it to operate a cylinder linked to the gun's action. It's actually no more efficient mechanically than recoil operation, and it requires meticulous cleaning to stay in top working order, but a gas-actuated system has a significant advantage over any other in noticeably reducing felt recoil.

Not pure recoil, mind you. Pure recoil is an immutable physical phenomenon governed by the weight of the gun, the weight of the ejecta, the weight of the powder charge, and the velocity it generates. With a given gun and load, the amount of recoil energy that's generated is exactly what we get, regardless of the action or how it works. What a gas system does is extend recoil over a longer period of time. A gas gun kicks just as hard as any other, but because the energy curve peaks more slowly, the kick doesn't feel as intense. And that alone is of immeasurable benefit to people who couldn't shoot as much, as well—or even at all—with harder-kicking guns.

You can find no better shotshells in the world than the best that are manufactured in the United States. Even the foreign-made cartridges that are equally as good as American best—I'm thinking particularly of the splendid shells made in Italy by Baschieri & Pellagri—are as good as they are in part because of an American invention.

Remington Arms introduced the one-piece polyethylene shotcup wad in 1960, and it changed the nature of shotshells forever. This simple little item made cartridges more efficient than they'd ever been. Its collapsible midsection cushions the shot charge at the moment of ignition; its deep obturating skirt seals the bore so that all the gas from the powder stays behind the shot charge; and its thick shotcup petals protect the outer pellets from being ground flat-sided against the barrel wall. All this means more ballistically useful pellets in a swarm traveling at consistently optimal velocity.

It also means that choke, which was invented to compensate for inefficient cartridges, has become virtually obsolete—even though a lot of shooters aren't yet ready to accept that notion.

What's more historically important is that everyone followed Remington's lead. Winchester introduced the AA wad in 1964, Federal its excellent Champion soon after. And now there are good shotcup wads in all but the cheapest of shells, no matter where they're made. For ammunition, these are truly the best of times.

For guns, too, though the evolution has taken somewhat longer. And as with most things technical, the significance, or even the nature, of these inventions may not be as apparent to everyone as they are to you and me. Like, for instance, the lady who some years ago worked on the editorial staff of a well-known sporting magazine. Preparing a photo-shoot to illustrate a story, they had several guns in the office. She picked up one of them and asked what it was.

It's a gas-operated autoloader, someone told her.

She looked it over and in a supremely reasonable tone asked, "Okay, where do you put in the gas?"

6

Rediscovered Treasure

Writing in 1928, Captain Charles Askins said: "The 20 bore is a specialty arm, rarely the size to be selected by the individual who is confined to one gun."

From about 1950 to the mid-80s, nearly everyone who wrote anything about shotgunning declared the 20-gauge the perfect all-around gun, the most versatile gauge ever, the best possible choice for everything from snipe to geese, on and on, ad nauseam.

Going from Okay to The Ultimate in less than a generation is quite a transformation, and you have to wonder what happened that improved the 20-bore so much in so short a time. There are two answers to this: One is "better ammunition," and the other is "nothing."

Captain Askins was speaking the truth of his time (he also said some things about the 20 that are true of all time, and I'll get to those presently). In the early days, guns that fired relatively small charges of shot simply were not very efficient, because cartridges were not very efficient. Even the best propellants literally blasted the shot charge down the bore, crushing a lot of pellets in the process. This began to change in the 1920s as Western Cartridge Company developed progressive-burning powders that didn't brutalize the shot quite so much, but shot columns, unprotected by any sort of collar, still scraped along the barrel wall so that all the pellets on the circumference ended up as misshapen, useless flyers.

These phenomena affected all the gauges, of course, but they were especially critical to the smaller ones and were the key factors in limiting the 20-bore's usefulness. The good Captain's reservations were not without good reason.

The 20-gauge didn't really come into its own until after 1960, when cartridge makers came up with the polyethylene shotcup wads that literally revolutionized shotgunning. By then, the 20 was already being hailed as the harbinger of a new era—and there was good reason for that, too.

With only a couple of exceptions, none of the great American double guns survived World War II, and only one survived past 1950. Even though repeaters were cheaper to manufacture than doubles, production costs became a crucial issue after the war, and gunmakers decided that building each gauge to true scale was no longer economical. Few built 28s and .410s on scaled actions to begin with, and no one was making 10-gauge repeaters, so there was nothing to discard on those fronts. It was the 16, long the upland gunner's darling, that got the axe. Machining actions in two sizes was obviously cheaper than three, so the manufacturers kept a big one and a little one, 12 and 20, and dropped the one in the middle. Thereafter, 16-gauges were built on 12-bore actions—which is why the 16 all but disappeared—and all the smallbores were built on 20s.

Having solved a manufacturing problem, the gun industry then set about solving a marketing problem: how to persuade hunters that 20-bores were better than their traditional 16s.

In fact, it wasn't difficult. The GIs who came home from the war were already infatuated with sheer firepower, so repeaters naturally appealed to them. Having had their fill of M1s and BARs and other heavy weapons, lightweight sporting arms were naturally appealing, as well. As for the rest, the manufacturers applied a little hype here and some new loads there, and the 20-gauge soon emerged as the be-all and end-all of shotguns.

Actually, the bull manure got shoveled in staggering proportions. Open a few gun magazines from the 1960s and '70s and you'll find a litany of sonorous pronouncements on the 20-bore's fabulous versatility, claims that range from marginally silly to utterly outrageous. Seldom in history has the outdoor press bought and then resold a more outlandish bill of goods.

Encouraged every step of the way, of course, by the arms and ammunition industry. Buzzwords and slogans once applied to the 16 (You Can Load It Up Like a 12 or Down Like a 20) now became the battle cry of the 20-gauge crusade. What came of that were some of the worst cartridges ever produced. Trying to load a 16 "up like a 12" is bad enough; attempting the same thing with a 20 is sheer disaster. The three-inch 20-gauge shell was nothing new—it had been around since the turn of the century—but never has a single cartridge been flogged with more vigor than that one was.

It conjured images of firepower, magnum mania, blood and guts, everything the gun and cartridge makers hoped for, and then some. Eventually, shooters who stopped to think seriously and question both their ballistics and ungodly recoil turned away from the miserable damn things, but by then a certain backlash had set in. Nothing exceeds quite like excess, and the excesses heaped upon the 20-gauge turned some shooters off altogether.

I was one of them. Some of the best guns I owned during the '60s and '70s were 20-bores, and even though my flirtation with the three-inch shell was mercifully brief (I'm not all that quick, but I really don't have to be hit by very many sledge hammers to pick up on a message), there were so few truly good ⅞-ounce field loads available that I finally wrote the 20-bore off as a lost cause and divided my shooting between the 12 and the 28. I would've gone back to a 16, but the ammunition scene was even more dismal there.

Captain Askins, 1928: "All [20-gauge] guns should shoot either an ounce or ⅞ ounce, nothing heavier or lighter. Dr. Carver once had a 20 bore built for 1¼ ounces of shot, 7½ pounds of arm, 3½-inch cases—that is one form of foolishness. A lot of us have had feather weight twenties chambered for 2½ inch cases, shooting ¾ ounce of shot, which is another form of foolishness."

He was right for all time about the heavy loads, right only for his own about the light ones.

I'll also go along partway with his assessment of gun weight: "All [20-gauge] guns should weigh from 6 to 6¾ pounds, neither heavier nor lighter." Six pounds is about the minimum I can handle consistently well, regardless of gauge, but in a game gun, 6½ pounds is to my mind tops for a 20. Beyond that, it might as well be a 12.

Despite what you might read to the contrary, the 20 is not the most versatile gauge. The 12-bore is. Overload a 20 and it is a poor-shooting instrument of torture; give it a load suited to the best nature of the gun, and it's a gem. A ⅞-ounce charge is optimal. A 20 can still shine on a one-ounce diet, but reduce the ration to ¾ ounce and it really shines.

My path back to the 20-bore fold started about ten years ago, with an unpretentious but wonderfully good-handling Ugartechea boxlock gun and a case of Estate Cartridge's Mighty-Lite shells. The gun is possibly the best value in a side-by-side you can find anywhere, and the cartridges are magnificent: ¾ ounce of good hard shot that performs in a very short string. On quail, grouse, woodcock, and birds of similar size, they're every bit as deadly as they are comfortable to shoot.

Virtually every cartridge maker now has excellent ⅞- and one-ounce 20-gauge field loads, and just recently I found yet another: a ⅞ ounce load made by Olympia for Poly-Wad and marketed as the Hornet. I shot half a case of them at clays and quail at Rockfence Station in Alabama, and in the end there was virtually no residue left in the barrels. I like clean, especially when it's a secondary benefit to first-rate performance—and perform they do.

I might have remained on the outskirts of the 20-gauge world forever, content to dabble where I once delved deeply, but for Tony Galazan's determination to bring back the A.H. Fox. Having written a 400-page book and Lord knows how many thousand magazine words on the subject, it's no secret that I believe the Fox is the best of all American double guns. Since 1995, I have taken my new Fox 20 all over the United States, to Mexico and South America, and have used it for everything from pheasants and sharptails to quail and doves. It has served to remind me how truly sweet a 20-bore can be.

Smallbores, especially, suffer from being too short at the business end. Captain Askins again: "All [20-gauge] guns should have either 28 inch or 26 inch barrels, neither longer nor shorter." But, he goes on to say, "with weight enough . . . to steady the shooter it is as good a gun as anybody needs." The problem with most short-nosed 20s, as with short-nosed guns of any gauge, is that the weight is usually in the wrong place. The only way weight can "steady the shooter" is to put enough of it in his leading hand to make the gun swing smoothly. My Fox 20 has 30-inch barrels, and nobody who has ever picked it up has complained that it felt sluggish. In fact, at just over 6¼ pounds, it feels so lively that some have refused to believe the barrels really are 30 inches until we've measured them to prove it.

I don't plan to give up my 12-bores for late-season pheasants and the occasional duck, and you couldn't pry me loose from my favorite 28-gauge with a crowbar, but for all-around upland work I have to say the Captain was more right than wrong in suggesting that a good 20 is as much as any-one needs—especially if you don't ask more of it than it can reasonably deliver. But there's hardly any need for that, because what it can deliver is lovely indeed.

7

THE 28-GAUGE
RENAISSANCE

Jack O'Connor thought there was no excuse for it; Elmer Keith believed it could be "a real gun"; Captain Askins said if he had one that would shoot hundred-percent patterns at 20 yards he'd mount a peep-sight on it and use it a lot; and several generations of American gunners largely ignored it altogether.

Given the underwhelming impression it made for so long, it's a wonder the 28-gauge still exists—and perhaps an even greater wonder that now, at last, it's finally coming into its own.

Or perhaps not. The 28-gauge's capabilities haven't changed much in the past 30 years. What has changed, and relatively recently, is that both cartridge- and gunmakers have come to take the 28-bore seriously, and that's happened because a new generation of shooters has discovered what some of us have thought for yearst—that the 28 is in many ways the ideal smallbore.

Time was, writers and shooters talked of the 28 and .410 in the same breath, as if they were virtually ballistic twins. I've always had a notion those

---

were people who'd never spent much time actually shooting a 28, or if they had, it was with one of the monumentally poor-handling guns that's all too often been the 28-bore's most common incarnation.

Fact is, the 28 and .410 aren't even in the same phylum, much less the same family or genus. The .410's bore is simply too narrow to fire any decent amount of shot in anything but a strung-out swarm with enough gaps to throw a sackful of poodles through.

But take a bore that measures .550-inch, feed it a perfectly balanced shot charge, and magic begins to happen. Ammunition makers once thought a ⅝ ounce load was optimal in a 28-gauge, but in the 1930s they discovered that a ¾ ounce charge strikes an ideal proportion between the height of the shot column and the diameter of the bore. You'll sometimes hear this described as a "square" load, although it's a bit misleading; a ¾ ounce charge in a 28-gauge case is slightly longer than its diameter—but not so much longer as to be intrinsically inefficient.

This means the 28-bore produces a very short shot string, scarcely more than three feet, as opposed to the .410's typical seven- to 12-foot string. Or to put it another way, a ¾-ounce charge doesn't contain a lot of pellets—only about 300 No. 8s, for instance—but they all reach the target at pretty much the same time. With high-quality cartridges carrying extra-hard shot in a good shotcup wad, it is one of the most ballistically efficient shotshells ever devised. If you want to see a bird die like it's been struck by lightning, center it with a 28-bore at any distance out to 35 yards or a bit beyond.

Inevitably, the 28 got its share of abuse from the more-is-better fallacy, just like all our other gauges. Years ago, Federal produced a ⅞ ounce load that ultimately proved to be not one whit better than the ¾ ounce charge. Elmer Keith's grudging compliment toward the 28 was, not surprisingly, predicated on the one-ounce loads that both Federal and Winchester made for a while in the late 60s. Winchester re-introduced this bit of nonsense a few years ago as its so-called Magnum one-ounce 28-gauge. I saw no sense in it at the time and see even less now that I've shot a couple cases of them. Overload a 28-bore and the same thing happens as when you overload any gauge—more recoil, more shot-stringing, less efficiency. Anything beyond a ¾-ounce charge is, in a word, worthless.

(This is not to say you can't get good 28s from either company. Federal's Gold Medal Sporting Clays round, loaded with No. 8½ shot, is excellent, and Winchester's AA, with newly available No. 8 shot, has become my favorite 28-gauge game load. Both carry ¾-ounce of shot ahead of proper 2-dram-equivalent powder charges.)

Parker built the first American double guns in 28-gauge, beginning about 1905. Ithaca followed in 1911 with a 28-bore version of the Flues Model double and, after 1925, of the New Ithaca Double. Neither A.H. Fox, Lefever, L.C. Smith, nor Baker ever put 28s into production, but many of the other great American gunmakers did. Winchester chambered both the Model 12 and Model 21 for the little cartridge. Remington introduced the first autoloading 28-gauge, the Model 11-48, in 1952, and Browning the first factory over/under in 1960.

Virtually none of the factory-built 28s were built on true 28-gauge frames. Sales simply couldn't justify the expense of tooling up machinery to produce completely scaled-down guns, so nearly all of them amount to 28-gauge barrels on 20-gauge frames. The same thing happened to the 16-gauge after World War II—16-bore barrels on 12-bore frames—and for the same reason. Both gauges' popularity subsequently declined as shooters decided, rightly enough, that if they had to have a gun that weighed as much as a 20 or a 12, it might as well be a 20 or 12 and not some bastardized in-between hybrid.

The short-barrel jag American gunners went on after the war didn't help either. The sporting press, including a lot of gun writers who should have known better, for some reason decided that short barrels were the greatest thing since canned beer, all without any regard for balance and handling. Their readers bought into it whole-hog, and the arms industry began cranking out some of the worst-handling guns ever built.

This was especially true of the smallbores and of the 28-gauge in particular, because the thinking of the time had it that the smaller the gauge, the smaller the gun should be. Short-nosed, muzzle-light guns were touted as being lightning-quick to start moving after a target. And they are—but they're just as easy to stop. The lighter and shorter the gun, the harder it is to control and to swing smoothly. The more weight you subtract from the barrels, the more jumpy and jittery a gun becomes, and consistent shooting suffers as a result.

It's not the cartridge's fault that a six-foot, 170-pound man can't shoot worth a damn with a four-pound gun that's scarcely longer than his arm, but the 28 took a black eye among a lot of bird shooters because of it.

It's fair to say that if there were no 28-gauge event in skeet there probably would no longer be a 28-gauge at all, and it was skeet shooters who first realized what a lovely thing the cartridge is when fired in something that more resembles a real gun than a toy. In fact, a lot of skeeters found their averages to be higher with the 28 than with any other gauge, and the reasons for that are perfectly simple: At the distances where skeet targets (and most upland birds) are shot, the ⅛ ounce difference in shot charge between 20-gauge and 28 is utterly meaningless, but the 28 generates considerably less recoil, so you can fire literally hundreds of shots in a day without getting a case of the flinches and yips.

Game shooters who tried 28-bores of similar proportion got similarly pleasing results, and because of them and the sporting clays shooters who dig smallbores, we're now in the midst of a renaissance. More new 28-bore guns and loads have come on the market in the past four or five years than have appeared in the past four or five decades.

And some of the guns are real 28-bores, perfectly scaled in every dimension to fit the barrels' slender grace. Beretta's Model 687EL Gold Pigeon Field was the first factory-built over/under made to true 28-gauge scale, followed last year by Ruger's 28-bore version of the excellent Red Label. The Merkel 147E is a nicely proportioned side-by-side. And the magnificent new A.H. Fox, built by Connecticut Shotgun Manufacturing Company, is now available in true 28-gauge as well. Any of the best English makers will of course be happy to build a 28 to your specifications, either side-by-side or over/under.

To my thinking, the best values of all are the fine sidelock ejector side-by-sides you can have made to order in Spain, by Arrieta, AyA, and Garbi. At less than $5,000 (for some models, a lot less), these guns cannot be beat—and as 28-bores they truly shine, because they're made in perfect proportion.

Whatever maker you choose, I promise you'll be happiest if you ignore the old nonsense about short barrels and light guns and get one that feels like a gun rather than a pool cue. A lot of those old short-nosed pieces are still out there on the market and they're ideal for a youngster or a lady (in fact, the 28-gauge is the perfect starter gun for any new shooter), but if you're a man of average size or larger, make it a full-sized gun. Have the stock made or altered to fit you, and have the barrels at least 28 inches, longer if you can.

Sounds like heresy, I know, given the gospel as it has been writ for the past 50 years, but it's the straight skinny from somebody who's been there and back. My favorite 28-gauge, which is well on its way to becoming my favorite game gun, is a round-body sidelock ejector that Arrieta built for me a couple of years ago. It has a 15¼-inch stock, 29-inch barrels, and weighs six pounds—and I'll bet it against all the stray feathers and brush chaff in your game pouch that if you swung it a couple of times you'd want to shoot it, and if you shot it, you'd love it.

And if you're skeptical about the 28-gauge in general, find a gun that fits and one that really swings, get a couple boxes of good ¾ ounce cartridges, shoot it for a month at any game smaller than pheasants, and just see if you don't find the magic.

8

THE ONE I LOVE
TO HATE

I'll confess at the start that I have an extremely bad attitude toward the .410. I hate the bloody thing, despite the fact that I shot my first quail and rabbit with one. Not even the memory of how my grandfather, whom I adored, called his a "four hundred and ten" is enough to soften the contempt I feel for that wretched little misfit masquerading as a shotgun.

The damn thing isn't even a proper gauge, as we traditionally define our guns; it's a bore-size, a scrawny little pipe .410-inch in inside diameter, and there's just no excuse for it.

Now, having got that off my chest, I also have to say that the .410 has an interesting history, can be a beautiful gun, and is sometimes really fun to shoot.

The .410 shotshell is an American invention that began with the .44 Winchester Center Fire rifle cartridge. Around the turn of the twentieth century, ammunition makers began loading the .44 WCF—or .44-40, as it's

---

more popularly known—with a capsule of shot, mainly for use in such pieces as the Marble's Game Getter and the Stevens Pocket Shotgun. Because both were premiums that could be earned by selling tins of Cloverine Salve, they were first guns for a lot of American boys, and the availability of shot as well as bulleted cartridges just made them that much more versatile and desirable.

The .44-40 Shot presently evolved into the .44 XL, a longer case capable of holding more pellets. The XL, which I presume stood for "Extra Long," wasn't very efficient, but it became extremely popular—largely, I suspect, because it was factory-loaded as a shotshell while the 2½-inch .44-65 version never was.

Both the .44-40 Shot and .44 XL were loaded in brass cases. Inevitably, about 1911, someone devised a paper shotshell in the .40-caliber range. Exactly who did it is probably forever lost in history, but someone came up with the notion of loading a two-inch German 12mm gas cartridge with about ⅜ ounce of shot and reducing bore diameter to .410-inch, and thus the .410 was born.

The 12mm designation refers to chamber diameter, incidentally, and .410 shotshells made in Europe before about 1930 were customarily head-stamped "12mm." Ballistically, they weren't much better than the brass-cased .44s, so it was also inevitable that someone would think to lengthen the case. Birmingham Small Arms claims to have in 1913 built the first guns, bolt-actions, chambered for a 2½-inch case. The Stevens Model 106 single-shot was the first American gun chambered for the same cartridge, followed by Winchester's Model 20 in 1919 and Model 41 in 1920.

I believe Parker was the first American maker to build .410 double guns, about 1927. Eventually, of course, they all did, except A.H. Fox and Lefever Arms. Winchester introduced its Model 42 pump gun, and the three-inch cartridge, in 1933.

None of the American double-gun makers built .410s in great numbers, so they're highly sought-after by collectors. They are also somewhat problematic, because none was made to true .410 proportion. Tooling up machinery to mill tiny frames and lock parts for guns that sold in comparatively minuscule numbers simply was not cost-effective. The same was true of 28-bores.

So, the factories chose the more economical course of building 28s and .410s on 20-gauge frames—which is why American 28-gauges look disproportionately bulky and the .410s often look downright weird. Guns that were built on relatively small frames to begin with—L.C. Smith, for instance— aren't so bad as .410s. A.H. Fox Gun Company, which made the smallest of all American boxlock frames, never made 28s or .410s, but Connecticut Shotgun has built some new Foxes in both over the past couple of years, using what is essentially a 20-gauge frame, and they both strike me as being the most handsomely proportioned of American sub-bores.

To my eye, the big-framed guns, Ithaca and Parker, are impossibly clunky looking as .410s. Parker's No. 0, 00, 000 frames—used for 20s, 28s, and .410s, respectively—actually are all the same size, although they do differ in weight. To its credit, Parker Brothers went farther than any of the others in attempting to at least make the sub-bore frames lighter, by milling a certain amount of steel out of the water table to create the No. 00 and 000 frames. It does help the handling quality a bit, but doesn't do a thing for appearance. Visually, Parker .410s do not turn me on.

On the other hand, I am by no means immune to the dainty grace of a .410 whose frame is in true proportion to its barrels. Much as I dislike ultra-light guns, show me a well-dimensioned .410 by one of the best English or European makers, and I'll get as gooey over it as anybody. Perfect symmetry is perfect symmetry, regardless of how large or small something happens to be, and I'm a goner for that.

In fact, I've seen a couple of .410s over the past few years that even made me wish I owned them. At the 1999 Safari Club show, Scottish maker David McKay Brown showed me one of his splendid round-action over/unders built as a .410, and if I'd had the money I would've bought it on the spot. A year or two earlier, I had the pleasure of shooting the first Holland & Holland Royal over/under ever built in .410, and I liked that one, too, both for its exquisite proportions and for the fact that I could actually hit something with it on a fairly regular basis. I didn't get to shoot McKay Brown's gun, but it had the same feel, as if a man could swing it with some genuine measure of control.

Among American guns, if you take away the single-shots, only Winchester's sweet little Model 42 pump is the real .410 quill in terms of size; that and the fact that they were invested with all of the old-time Winchester quality is why they now fetch such ungodly high prices. Beretta currently makes a .410 over/under that also is truly proportioned.

My distaste for the .410 has nothing to do with the gun, so long as it's properly built, but I detest the .410 cartridge. I've spilled enough words on the phenomena of shot-stringing and the fallacy of overloads that I won't rehash it again, except to say that the .410 is without question the absolute worst combination of shot charge and bore size of all our standard shotguns. It's not the worst possible; the European 6mm and 9mm rimfire shotshells own that dubious distinction. But of what you can buy in the typical American gunshop or hardware store, you cannot find anything more ballistically lousy than a box of .410s, regardless of whether it's the standard 2½-inch skeet load or the three-inch version.

If you understand even the basics of shotgun ballistics, the reason why is obvious: There simply is no such thing as a shot charge that is both balanced and useful in a bore that small. For a tube only ⁴/₁₀s of an inch, an optimal load—one in which the length of a shot column is proportional to its diameter—is only about a quarter-ounce, certainly no more than the original ⅜-ounce. That's not enough shot to produce consistently dense patterns at any but the closest range.

Adding pellets to a shot column without increasing its diameter soon reaches a point of diminishing returns, and with a .410 it doesn't take much before the returns start diminishing drastically. There's so little space in that pencil-sized bore that a huge proportion of pellets are in contact with the barrel wall. Unprotected, these will become useless flyers once they leave the muzzle—but adding a nice, thick shotcup to protect them reduces the circumference of the shot column even more, making it that much longer and skinnier yet.

This, in turn, promotes shot stringing, and stringing is the .410's worst characteristic of all. It's a flaw inherent to a long shot column—and in order to get any useful number of pellets into such a narrow space, a long column is the only kind you can have. That means the shot are relatively strung out even in the cartridge, so by the time the swarm reaches a target twenty-odd yards away, the leading pellets may be fifteen feet or more ahead of those bringing up the rear. Having so few of them in the charge to begin with, that long a string produces enormous gaps in the pattern.

As with any stringing, it does less mischief to straightaway or oncoming shots, but crossing targets can pass right through the swarm without encountering enough pellets for a clean break or kill—or without encountering any at all. If you want to see the tale told in graphic terms, just look at the annual averages in registered skeet. Among shooters who participate in every event, their averages with the .410 will be the lowest of all. Fact is, you can make a dead-perfect shot with the little gun and still fail to break, or even hit, a target.

That's the inherent weakness in the cartridge, and what to my mind disqualifies the .410 as a serious game gun. It's not that you can't kill birds with one, but you can't do it consistently or reliably. The .410 is a sow's ear that not even the best ammunition makers can turn into a silk purse. It's a crippler, and crippling shouldn't be anyone's idea of good sport.

I have in my files magazine articles from the 1950s and '60s that extol the virtues of the .410 for every game up to and including turkeys, and if I had a dollar for every time some fool has blithely pronounced it perfect for a beginning shooter, I could buy one of McKay Brown's round-actions and have some cash left over. A .410 is, in fact, the worst gun you could possibly give a beginner, way too difficult to shoot well and the antithesis of the confidence-building a beginner needs.

If you're a seasoned shot, skeet with a .410 can be a hoot—provided you're philosophical enough to accept the fact that you can do everything right and still see targets sail off unscathed or merely nicked. It's one of the few situations when you truly can blame some misses on the gun.

Watching a game bird fly away merely nicked is a different story. That can happen with any gun, of course, but going after tough, strong wild birds with a .410 is just asking for it. Wounding and losing a bird because of a poor shot weighs heavily enough on my conscience; I'd rather not court the feeling of losing one because I made a good shot with a poor cartridge.

My attitude about all this has earned me more than one bollocking from the .410's more vocal apologists. Which is okay; everyone's entitled to an opinion, even one as indefensible as calling the .410 a good cartridge. By the same token, everybody deserves a pet peeve, something upon which to vent one's spleen—and for that I'll take the .410, any time.

9

SMALLBORES AND SPORTSMANSHIP

$\mathbf{M}$any years ago, a couple of friends and I were hunting quail in Texas, sharing a lodge with some people we didn't know. One of them came into the gunroom one morning just as I was taking my 12-gauge John Wilkes off the rack. He looked at it.

"Guess you like to shoot 'em with a cannon, huh?" The tone was not unfriendly, but there was no mistaking the hint of superiority in it, nor in his little smile.

I replied with a noncommittal, "Huuummh?"

"That there cannon you got. Me, I shoot a 20—more sportin' for these little ol' quail."

"Ah."

"Yeah, more sportin' when you don't shoot no big ol' gun," he went on, rummaging under the bench and setting out his shells. I looked at the boxes: One-ounce 20s.

"Oh, the way I shoot, I need all the help I can get," I said, dumped a

---

couple of boxes of ⅞-ounce handloads into my shell bag, wished him a good hunt, and went out to join my partners on the truck.

That was neither the first nor the last time I've heard the opinion that smallbore guns are more sportsmanlike. Shotgunning, in fact, may be the only predominantly male pastime in which smaller is so often thought of as better. I've seen hunters carrying 28-bores sneer at 16s, and guys with 20s look at a 12-gauge as if it was something they'd just scraped off their boots. And some .410 aficionados—talk about an attitude with ears.

I know where this comes from. Part of it is inexperience or a misunderstanding of how shotguns really work, and part of it has to do with a certain view of sportsmanship.

The American concept of sportsmanship derives from the English notion that participating with good grace and good character is more important than the outcome. Or as my father used to tell me, it's not whether you win or lose, but how you play the game—an idea that seems to have become quaintly old-fashioned in American team sports and among certain tennis players.

Not taking an unfair advantage is another aspect of English sportsmanship that Americans adopted, and this one has particular relevance to the field sports. It explains why fly-fishermen cast devices made from hair, yarn, and feathers instead of worms or kernels of Green Giant corn—and why shooting a bird on the ground or the water or out of a tree is repugnant to most bird hunters. Allowing an animal the full extent of its physical and mental capacities to elude or escape, essentially serves the notion of fair chase.

True, we use dogs, decoys, calls, camouflage, blinds, and all manner of other assistance that could arguably be indicted as unfair advantage, but these are traditional in our sport and function more to provide opportunities than to ensure success. If these truly did amount to unfair advantage, then anyone who used them would be successful every time. That we so often come home empty-handed despite it all strikes me as sufficient evidence to the contrary.

This is where the question of smallbores comes in—and where it seems to me a matter of sportsmanship gone astray.

With one exception, I can't see that the gun itself has the slightest thing to do with sportsmanship. Intrinsically, a gun is neither sporting nor unsporting; in the end, it is simply a tool that a hunter can use in a sporting or unsporting way. To my mind, sportsmanship resides solely in my decisions about how and when I use my gun, in whether I choose to take this shot or not take that one, in the choice of whether to shoot a covey of quail on the ground or a grouse in a popple tree or to wait until they're on the wing.

To carry this a step further: If after exercising my own principles of sportsmanship I decide it's a shot I'm willing to take, I want that bird stone dead as quickly and efficiently as possible. In that moment, we each possess our so-called sporting chance; it has its wings and its habitat, I have my gun. I want either a clean kill or a clean escape, and if we've both done our best, it really doesn't matter which it turns out to be.

Now, about the exception I mentioned earlier: I do think there's one valid issue of sportsmanship that does involve the gun itself. Personally, I consider it highly unsportsmanlike to use a gun that is inadequate to the task. I know you can kill any bird at almost any distance with a lucky shot from any gun; what I'm talking about is a gun that lacks the intrinsic capacity to produce a clean kill for every reasonable opportunity.

I insist upon giving the bird a sporting chance to surprise, baffle, out-maneuver, or otherwise thwart my attempt on its life, but that does not include the possibility that it will fly off wounded half the time, even when I put the shot charge right where it belongs. That, to me, is as distasteful, and disgraceful, as ground-swatting a woodcock.

In practical terms, this means I don't hunt any game bird with a .410. It also means I don't hunt ducks or prairie grouse or late-season pheasants with a 28-bore—nor with cartridges of any gauge that can't deliver sufficient energy for a reliable kill out to the greatest distance at which I'm willing to take my shots.

This stipulation aside, I can't for the life of me see how a smallbore is any more "sporting" than a larger one. An ounce of shot is an ounce of shot, regardless of whether you fire it through a 20-gauge, a 16, or a 12. The larger bores will perform a bit more efficiently, but they'll all handle a one-ounce load well enough that a bird wouldn't know the difference.

Part of the problem stems from a still-common assumption that a large-bore gun must fire a big shot charge. Had I bothered to point out to my Texas acquaintance that I was shooting less shot in my 12 than he was in his 20, the response probably would have gone something like, "Well, what the hail good is a puny little ol' load like that in a twailve-gauge?" In the face of that kind of thinking, you're damned if you do and damned if you don't.

What it really boils down to, I'm afraid, is that a surprising number of people truly believe there's a direct relationship between the size of a gun barrel and the size of the shot pattern you get out of it. There's a specious sort of logic to the notion that the shot swarm from a 28-gauge ought to be smaller in diameter than one from a 12-gauge. You can explain that the large-bore pattern is likely to be denser because it comprises more pellets but that, chokes being equal, the two will be so nearly identical in spread as to make no practical difference—but don't be surprised if a lot of shooters refuse to believe it till they see it on a patterning plate. And I suppose there are some, who know what they know and aren't about to be sidetracked by facts, who wouldn't believe it even then.

Given this as the basis for a conviction that smallbores are more "sporting," it's not hard to understand why those who are most committed to that belief are also those most likely to stuff ungodly quantities of shot down their sporty little guns. They're usually the ones who insist on shooting 12-gauge loads in 20-bores and 16-gauge loads in 28s. Such bet-hedging seems to me a tacit admission that they don't really have much confidence in their smallbores—sporty is sporty, but you have to draw the line some-where, after all.

All this is thoroughly misguided, of course, but innocent enough in the end. Overloads are ballistically atrocious, but if you're going to err one way or the other, it's probably better to have too much shot in the air than not enough. The birds that do get hit usually end up pretty well anchored, and if getting the snot kicked out of him every time he pulls the trigger makes somebody feel like a sport, it's okay with me.

But the whole silly notion of the "sporty" smallbore does have a down-side, because it poisons the well for those who might otherwise pursue the genuine delights of a small-gauge gun.

To illustrate: Not long ago, I had some correspondence with a very nice chap who'd had just enough experience with the 28-gauge to be intrigued by it and who asked for some advice in choosing a good 28-bore gun. He never once mentioned thinking it might be "more sporting," and he struck me from the start as being too bright to buy into such nonsense anyway. But after we'd exchanged two or three letters, he said his first experience with a 28 had "forced a concentration" on his part, and thus revealed his misgivings—not that the gun might be inadequate to the game but rather that he might be inadequate to the gun.

Although it's slowly fading, there still is a widespread tendency to view the 28-gauge—and in some quarters, the 20—as little more than a popgun. A great many who don't necessarily see it as "sporting" certainly do see it as a serious handicap.

It's the old misconception based on size, reinforced by the myth of the "sporty" smallbore. When that slender little cartridge is still a largely unknown quantity, a shooter looks at it and almost inevitably concludes that actually hitting a moving object with such a wee thing must surely require the uttermost precision. And with that, he's all but doomed before he even begins.

Trying to be oh-so-precise is the antithesis of good, consistent shooting. It tempts you to aim rather than simply point, teases you into trying to measure your forward allowance—which means looking at the gun, which in turn is the ticket to missing behind, time after time...which only seems to confirm the original misconception.

A smallbore requires the same thing as any gun—an act of faith, a willingness to stay loose, stay focused on the target, just swing the gun and let 'er rip. With a smallbore, the results may at first seem like a fluke, or beginner's luck, but the longer you keep the faith, the sooner you'll convince yourself that within its practical limits, hitting and killing a bird is no more difficult with a little cartridge than with a big one.

And at that point, whatever notion you might've had about smallbores being "sporty" just by virtue of their size should be history. Of the birds I kill in a year's hunting, the majority, by far, come to bag at the behest of a 20 or a 28—not because I'm out to handicap myself but rather because I know they can do what I want them to do and are pleasant to carry and shoot, besides.

Even so, every time I take my 28-gauge to a lodge or a dove field, somebody invariably comments that I must be one whizbang shot to use such a little gun. I tell them not so, the gun's no handicap, that anybody can shoot a 28, but I don't think most of them really believe me. I have no objection if they want to think I'm the reincarnation of Lord Ripon, but I'd much prefer to put a good smallbore in their hands and help them see for themselves; would rather create a convert than be a counterfeit hero, any day.

10

THE VERSATILE GUN

Thirty years ago, it was the Grail. The gun and ammunition makers sold it to shooters, and we in turn sold the idea to our wives.

The versatile gun. The One. The be-all and end-all, the gun that will do everything from skeet to ducks. Whether by virtue of size, shape, action, or gauge, it was the gun that would suffice for every application to which we aspired. It was eminently practical—perhaps less eminently affordable, but what of that, considering it was The Last Gun We'll Ever Need?

It's an attractive notion, at least in theory: One high-quality gun, with a perfectly fitted stock, capable of serving a gunner's every purpose. There is, after all, something to the old adage about being ware of the man who shoots only one gun. Besides, when you come right down to it, anything that goes bang and flings a reasonable charge of shot will serve any gunning purpose up to a point. You can shoot quail with a trap gun, trap with a quail gun, grouse with a duck gun, skeet and clays with just about anything, and so on. Whether the gun will allow you to do any of these things well is the kicker, of course, but with that aside, the fact is, guns is guns and targets is targets.

You can easily build a case to argue that the versatile gun certainly does exist. Apart from such specialized pieces as pigeon and trap guns, all of mine, for instance, are virtually identical—similar in weight, barrel length, chokes, balance, stock dimensions, trigger pulls, whatever. They are versatile to the point that I can use any one of them for any game I happen to hunt, and I can shoot them all equally well.

Even so, they aren't all appropriate to every species of game because there are three different gauges involved—12, 20, and 28—and this is where the wheels start to come off the concept of versatility.

Versatile guns, yes; versatile gauges, not necessarily.

Time was, one of the standard arguments in favor of the 16-gauge is that you could "load it up like a 12 or down like a 20." After World War II, when for economic reasons the gun industry started touting the 20-bore as the greatest thing since canned beer, it was draped with a similar mantle of versatility. I don't recall anyone praising the 20 because you could load it up like a 16 or down like a 28—but only because the 16 was on a fast track toward obsolescence at the time, and because in those days nobody but skeet shooters cared a damn about the 28-gauge anyway.

The whole point of the loading-up-and-down business was, of course, versatility. Like most such concepts, there's a grain of truth in it, but it all soon went wrong in the face of the American penchant for believing that more is better. That meant loading up rather than down. Until very recent times, no American manufacturer ever has made factory 16-gauge cartridges with 20-gauge—that is, ⅞ ounce—loads. But you could always, and still can, find 16-bore cartridges stuffed with 12-gauge loads of 1⅛ or even 1¼ ounces of shot. In the 1960s and 70s, a few dingbats in the sporting press argued that the best way to save the ailing 16 was to make it available in a three-inch case. Mercifully, neither the gun nor ammunition industries paid any attention—mainly because they had no interest in rescuing the 16 in the first place. If they had, we probably would have seen three-inch 16s. They'd have been ballistically awful, but certainly better than the three-inch 20s that have been beating the snot out of shooters for close on to fifty years. (The three-inch 20 actually has been around for a century or more, but only in the past forty-odd years has it seen anything like widespread use.)

In reality, neither the 16 nor the 20 accommodates much latitude in terms of ammunition. No smallbore does, really, and they all respond better when they're under- rather than overloaded. A 16 is perfect with an ounce of shot. It'll perform reasonably well with 1⅛ ounces, just as a 20-bore can usually handle a full ounce fairly well. But if you want to depart from optimal loads and still make 'em really shine, try some ⅞ ounce 16s and ¾ ounce 20s. The shot strings are very short, patterns beautifully dense, recoil is slight, and they possess a killing power on game that is simply astonishing.

Among real game cartridges (a category that to my mind does not include the .410), the 28-gauge is most sensitive of all. Its standard ¾-ounce charge cannot be improved upon, not by the old ⅝-ounce load and certainly not by anything heavier. There used to be a ⅞-ounce factory load, but it faded away because it didn't perform well, and with any luck at all, the current one-ounce "magnum" 28 will go the same route.

Perhaps more than any other, the 28-bore points up the difference between a versatile gun and a versatile load. It is the least versatile of all in terms of shot charge, but for all-around upland hunting there isn't much its ¾-ounce of shot won't do perfectly well. I don't use it for late-season wild pheasants, nor for sharptails or prairie chickens, but it's my favorite for everything else, from ruffed grouse to bobwhites to doves to snipe. I've used it to good effect on ptarmigan and spruce grouse as well.

We do have one truly versatile gauge, and that's the 12. You can load it with anything from ¾ up to 1⅝ ounce, of shot and be confident of solid performance. The heaviest loads are brutally punishing in a lightweight gun, and the lightest loads cannot make a heavy gun feel lively, but if you want to run the ammunition gamut and still have good ballistics, a 12-bore is the only way to go.

The best thing to come out of two generations' preoccupation with the notion of versatility is that we're coming out of it. I know quite a few chaps who own only one or two guns, but it's because that's all their sense of family responsibility says they can afford, not because they buy into the notion that there's any such thing as one gun that can do it all. For them, the prospect of adding a 28-gauge or perhaps a lightweight 20 is a "someday" affair. Nothing wrong with that. Something to look forward to is part of the great triad of life, ranking right alongside something to do and someone to love.

(11)

SOME OLD WIVES' TALES OF GUNNING

According to my copy of *Webster's*, a traditional belief that is not based in fact is called an old wives' tale. I don't know exactly how the phrase originated—it's been part of our language since at least the 16th century—nor whether it was meant to denote a tale told by an old wife or an old tale told by a wife. I don't even know what wives had to do with it in the first place, because I do know they aren't the only ones apt to pass along bits of popular wisdom that sound good but bear little burden of truth.

You know the sort of thing I'm talking about: A gun dog shouldn't be a pet; spaying a bitch makes her lose interest in hunting; on and on. I'll leave it to the dog guys on the staff to debunk those old wheezers; there are more than enough myths in guns and shooting to keep the gun guy occupied. Some are harmless enough, and it'd be a dull world without a few fancies here and there. But some others can actually interfere with both your skill and your enjoyment in shooting if you accept them as true—and the sooner those can be laid to rest, the better.

Of the former variety, my all-time favorite is the old notion that Some Guns Shoot Harder Than Others. This is often expressed by some grizzly-stubbled old-timer in reference to some wretched gaspipe that kicks the livin' bejeezus out of you every time you pull the trigger. The reasoning, I suppose, is that if a gun is nearly lethal at the back end, it has to be sheer death and destruction at the other.

Some guns actually do kick harder than others, even when fired with the same cartridges. Old American pieces, built in the days when stocks were commonly made with three or four inches of drop at the heel, are the worst culprits of all. Even a mild load in one of those old dog-legs can clear your sinuses in short order—but that doesn't mean the shot hits the bird with any more punch. More pellets may hit it, perhaps, because those same old guns were also bored tighter than an owl's butt in order to compensate for inefficient cartridges, but actual striking energy is solely a function of shot size and powder charge. Apart from choke, it has nothing whatever to do with the gun. Some cartridges shoot harder than others, but guns don't.

Not all gunning myths are so innocent. Like the one that says you can determine your proper stock length by tucking the butt into the crook of your elbow; if your finger falls comfortably onto the trigger, the length is right. I don't have a clue how this got started. It's so illogical that I can't even imagine how someone might have thought it up, but it's still floating around. Just a few weeks ago, I overheard a salesman in a very prestigious gun shop tell a customer that this is how stock fitters determine length of pull. He was serious about it, and the customer seemed to believe it.

Trust me, the length of your forearm hasn't the slightest thing to do with proper stock length. The full reach of your arm does, and so does the shape and mass of your shoulders and chest, but not your forearm alone. I'm not convinced that length, in and of itself, is as critical a dimension as some fitters think it is, but that's neither here nor there. The right length is whatever allows your cheek to touch the stock about three inches back from the base of your thumb, doesn't require that you roll your shoulder very far forward to make contact with the gun butt, and doesn't cause the butt to snag your armpit as you raise the gun to your face. There's no universal prescription, and certainly no connection with the length of your forearm.

A more modern, related myth has it that the adjustable triggers on high-tech target guns confer some latitude for adjusting stock length. Moving the trigger does change the measurement, because nominal length is measured from the trigger to the center of the butt. Practical length, however, is determined by the position of your trigger hand, and when you shoot a gun with a pistol grip, the grip dictates where your hand has to be. Being able to slide the trigger forward or back is dandy for accommodating the size of your hand and the length of your finger, but it doesn't change the practical length of the stock at all.

Over/unders and repeaters are sometimes said to be superior to side-by-sides because of their single sighting plane. This old saw has been around at least since the 1920s and probably longer, but it's sheer hogwash nonetheless. No gun has more than one "sighting plane," no matter how many barrels it has or how they're arranged. The insidious aspect of this myth is the implication that you "sight" a shotgun. You don't—at least not if you want to hit moving objects. You simply point it, just as you'd point a finger, and always with your eyes on the target. Look at the gun, and you'll slow or stop your swing, every time, guaranteed.

So, if you don't look at the gun, who gives a rat's patootie how many "sighting planes" it has? The fact is, if it fits and you handle it properly, it doesn't have any. It just shoots where you look.

In a similar vein, we American shooters have been indoctrinated for fifty years or more to believe that upland guns ought to have short barrels, especially for relatively small birds that flush at close range. And for hunting in the woods...well, Lordy me; to hear the old wives tell it, you'd think no grouse or woodcock hunter could possibly hit a bird unless his gun barrels scarcely reach past the forend, because anything longer is sure to get tangled in the brush.

Short barrels are not necessarily bad. My wife shoots short-barreled guns quite well—but she has to stretch to stand five-foot-one, and her proper stock length is exactly twelve inches. For me, six feet and stocked at better than fifteen inches, short barrels are a disaster. They're too light to give me any sense of being able to guide the gun smoothly and precisely along a target's flight line. And when the target is as small as a woodcock and as fleet as a quail, precise pointing is the difference between hits and misses.

Forget about short barrels being "best," and shoot what feels controllable. For men of average size, that means at least 28 inches, maybe even 30. I like 29 inches best of all.

I shoot 'em in the woods, too, and so can you. Think about the times when your gun ended up tangled in the alder shoots or popple sprouts, and tell me where you hit the snag. Was it just at the muzzles, or were you buried in some thicket so dense you'd have been hard-pressed to swing a .45 from the hip? Would three or four inches less barrel have made any difference? Probably not to the environment, but almost certainly to your ability to control the gun—and controlling the gun is what you need to do if you want to shoot effectively. Being at times unable to shoot at all is just part of the game, part of why it's called "hunting."

Everybody knows you need to use heavier shot late in the season because the birds have more feathers then, right? This is a myth based less on an understanding of ballistics than of biology. It's true that heavier shot packs more punch, but it's not true that late-season birds have any more feathers than they did on opening day. Most upland game birds undergo a molt right after the spring breeding season and grow a new set of feathers they'll wear till the following year. Wildfowl do this, too, but go through a second molt in late summer.

The point is that none of the game birds grow more feathers during the hunting season. They do get warier if they've been chivvied around by hunters and tend to flush at greater range, and that's a good reason to switch to heavier shot as the season wears on, to give yourself more reach with the killing energy of the pellets. Plumage itself, though, is not an issue.

Given the nature of myths, it shouldn't be surprising to find some that are specifically contradictory. (And not just in gunning; which is true, Absence Makes the Heart Grow Fonder or Out of Sight, Out of Mind?) In counterpoint to the notion of using larger shot to overcome denser late-season plumage, there's the old dictum that says small shot penetrates thick feathers better than big pellets.

Physics does not bear this out. Although the shape of a projectile does influence penetration to a minor extent, it's weight, not size, that makes the difference in comparing projectiles of the same shape and composition. Kinetic energy, which is a combination of mass and velocity, is what causes shot pellets to penetrate and kill, and if two pellets made of the same stuff are fired at the same velocity, the larger has the greater capacity for penetration; it's heavier, and the heavier a moving object, the greater its tendancy to keep moving.

Round objects shed velocity relatively quickly, which is why shotguns are short-range tools. The lighter the shot, the sooner it slows down, and the more it slows, the less penetrating energy it packs. Consequently, the charge of No. 7½ shot that'll kill a goose or duck stone dead at twenty yards is at fifty yards a crippler at best—just as the No. 4s that kill so cleanly at fifty yards are all but useless at eighty. The bottom line is that within its optimal energy range, any shot pellet will penetrate any suit of feathers and deliver a killing blow. Distance, not size alone, is the key.

Hang around shooters long enough, and you'll hear it said in all seriousness that women are afraid of guns and that a .410 is the ideal gun for a beginner. These myths truly make me cringe.

Some women are afraid of guns. Some people are afraid of snakes, and some men are afraid of women—but none were born that way. Fear is a learned response, based on conditioning. Properly shield a woman—or anyone else—from the painful noise of gunfire and from the brutal kick of a heavy load in a light gun, and she'll soon see there's nothing to fear, despite the boneheaded notions she was fed by her male colleagues, her imagination, or the news media.

But for heaven's sake, don't try to shield her by giving her a .410. And don't give one to your child, either. A .410 is not for a beginner; it's for a veteran shot who recognizes its truly awful ballistics and understands that it's the most difficult of all the standard cartridges with which to hit anything consistently. Nothing spurs interest like success, and nothing is more inimical to successful shooting than a .410 in the hands of a beginner. Any child who hasn't yet developed the upper-body strength to handle a 28- or 20-bore gun isn't physically ready to become a shooter. Far better to wait a year or two than trot out a .410 and thus influence a potential shooter to give it up forever.

As I said, some myths are harmless while others are not. Human nature being what it is, I doubt we can ever be wholly free of them, neither in gunning nor in the broader sense of life. But for all their persistence, there's one thing about old wives' tales that will be forever true: You don't have to believe them.

12

SIZE
MATTERS

Shotgunning is partly science, partly art, and partly compromise. A gun can be nearly perfect mechanically, and a shooter can be nearly perfect in the way he handles it, but there is always a certain shady zone where essentially contradictory elements have to be balanced against one another.

Weight, for instance. It's easy to say that a gun ought to be light enough to be dynamic but yet heavy enough to be optimally controllable and dampen recoil. It's also easy to identify the extremes; a guy who stands 6-foot-7 and has the muscles to bench-press an SUV isn't a good candidate for a five-pound gun, nor is a willowy woman likely to get along very well with one that weighs almost twice that much. It's the middle ground where things begin to get murky, and the ultimate answer is that you have to find what works best for you.

Perhaps the most important compromise in gunning has less to do with the gun than with the cartridge, particularly with the size of shot we choose.

Here, too, there are obvious extremes and a broad middle ground where contraries must be brought to balance.

A shot pellet is lethal in the same way as a bullet: It kills by transferring energy, which is created through the combination of mass and speed. Also like a bullet, the amount of energy a shot pellet carries is precisely quantifiable, governed by strict laws of physics, and is ultimately immune to alteration by wishful thinking or advertising hype.

A single pellet of any size, delivered directly to the brain with sufficient penetration, is capable of killing any game bird. But this, of course, is not how shotguns work. Shotguns depend upon multiple strikes delivering a cumulative amount of energy. And therein lies the rub.

The larger the pellet, the greater the energy—but on the other hand, the larger the pellet, the fewer of them are available in a given shot charge. The key to efficiency is finding a good balance between having enough pellets to ensure multiple strikes and having pellets large enough to generate sufficient energy for a reliably clean kill.

Pure logic suggests two simple solutions. One is simply to add more pellets to the charge. The other is to increase the speed—and therefore the energy—of smaller shot. Unfortunately, it's not quite that simple.

The interior diameter of a gun barrel determines the diameter of any shot column that can pass through it. Consequently, adding pellets to that column means increasing its length. That in turn increases the length of the shot string once the swarm is in the air, and the longer the string, the more blank spaces there are at any given point. If stuffing more shot down the pipe was any real advantage, the three-inch 20, the one-ounce 28, and a few other grotesquely overloaded rounds would be the cat's pajamas instead of a dog's breakfast.

Hyper speed isn't the answer, either, although we're still in the grips of a velocity fad that's been going on for several years. Somewhere in the double helix, there just seems to be a gene that refuses to believe that less can be more—because hard on the heels of a grudging admission that light shot charges are just as efficient as heavy ones, if not more so, cartridge makers started on a speed jag, cranking velocities of smaller shot charges to 1400 fps or more, thus trading one unnecessary excess for another.

Spend a few minutes studying a shot-pellet velocity and energy chart, and the fallacy becomes obvious. The faster you start a round projectile moving through the atmosphere, the faster it slows down. And the more it slows down, the more energy it sheds. A No. 6 pellet leaving a muzzle at 1200 fps, bearing 6.20 foot/pounds of energy, is moving 720 fps at 40 yards and packs energy of 2.23 foot/pounds. You can goose the muzzle velocity of the same pellet to 1330 fps and its muzzle energy to 7.62 foot/pounds, but at 40 yards it's only going 765 feet per second, and its energy is down to 2.52 foot/pounds.

In case you don't have a calculator handy, this means a difference of 130 fps and 1.42 foot/pounds energy at the muzzle amounts to only 45 fps and .29 foot/pounds at target distance. Does the faster load require less forward allowance? Sure, all of two or three inches less, which is not really something to get cranked up about when you're dealing with a pattern about three feet across. Does it deliver more killing power? Yes, but the difference is about enough to knock over a parakeet that wasn't feeling very well to begin with. Between the two loads, the only one who gets hit noticeably harder is the guy behind the gun.

Pharmaceutically, speed kills. In shotshell ballistics, excessive speed doesn't do diddly out where it counts.

Fact is, the efficiency of external ballistics involves a compromise between the size of the pellets and the number of them in a given charge.

Guns, birds, and the composition of shot all compound the dilemma. Pellets formed of pure lead have a wonderful mass and density, but they're too soft to escape being deformed when the powder ignites or when a charge is being driven down a barrel. Alloying lead with antimony and wrapping the charge in a polyethylene collar solves that problem, as does making pellets from iron, bismuth, tungsten-iron, tungsten-poly, or a compound of tungsten, nickel, and iron.

Birds are more problematic. Waterfowl, thickly feathered and strong-bodied, demand optimal penetration and a substantial amount of energy, which means large, heavy shot. Same for wild pheasants; their plumage isn't nearly as dense, but they're just too damn tough and mean to die quietly.

Guns are most problematic of all, because the loads they can handle most efficiently impose the most stringent limits. It is axiomatic that the more, and the larger, pellets you need to perform the job at hand, the larger the bore you ought to fire them through; what you're after is having enough pellets in a reasonably short column to ensure a short string and good pattern density.

The larger the bore, the more flexibility it offers. You can bump the standard ⅞-ounce 20-gauge load up to an ounce and still get good performance. Sixteens shine brightest with an ounce of shot, but most will behave well enough if they're given an eighth-ounce more, and the wonderfully versatile 12-bore typically is capable with any load up to an ounce and a half.

The same flexibility applies to pellet size as to quantity. As a rule, the larger the bore, the better it can handle larger shot. I've patterned quite a few 20s that didn't like anything larger than No. 6—and some that didn't even like 6s. My Fox 20 can print perfectly respectable patterns with No. 5 shot, but that's unusual in my experience.

Most of the 16s I've tested did just fine with No. 5s, but a fair number of them went patchy and inconsistent with 4s. I've seen very few 12-bores that didn't shoot lovely patterns with No. 4, but back in the old days when you could shoot lead at waterfowl and I was hunting geese a lot, I often had to tinker with my loads to get good patterns with No. 2. And in fact, I ended up trading off a couple of guns that just wouldn't shoot 2s worth a damn, no matter what I did.

Pheasants aren't the only upland birds that sometimes demand relatively large pellets. The prairie birds—sharptails, chickens, and Huns—can be spooky enough that if you don't take fairly long shots, you won't be taking many shots at all. None of them require as much hammering as pheasants do, but you still need pellets heavy enough to carry a reasonable amount of energy out to 40 or even 45 yards, and in numbers sufficient to make good, even patterns. To my thinking, an ounce of 6s is about the lightest reliable load for that kind of work. If I take a 20-gauge to the prairie, as I occasionally do, I have to be prepared to pass up some shots. More often, you'll find me out there with a 12-bore and 1⅛ ounce loads.

As you can see from the chart on page 82, the actual number of pellets you add to a charge in eighth-ounce increments isn't necessarily all that great—just under 30 of them in the case of No. 6—but with hard shot in a well-made cartridge, that's still 30 more pellets in the swarm, and 30 pellets can plug quite a few holes that might otherwise result in a fringy, crippling hit.

So why not shoot 1⅛ ounces of No. 7½ and have 393 pellets in the charge, as opposed to 253 No. 6s? The numbers are attractive, but the energy capability isn't. At 40 yards, a No. 7½ pellet that left the muzzle at 1200 fps only carries 1.26 foot/pounds of energy, almost a full foot-pound less than a No. 6 at the same speed. Just getting a pellet to arrive at a distant target is only part of deal; it also needs to get there still packing enough energy to deal a fatal blow.

No doubt you've noticed that I haven't said anything about my particular pet, the 28-gauge. (I have also not mentioned the .410-bore, but as this is an essay about game guns, I won't be going there.) Although a 28-gauge with ¾ ounce of shot can perform astonishingly well, it will only do so within a highly circumscribed set of limitations. It's the touchiest, pickiest gauge of all when it comes to shot size. I once owned a Ugartechea boxlock that could shoot No. 6s like gangbusters, and I once tested a Krieghoff that could do the same thing, but those are the only two 28s I've ever come across that would.

A ¾ ounce charge of No. 6 comprises 169 pellets, and if you want to see what a patchy pattern looks like, shoot one of those little suckers at 25 or 30 yards. It ain't pretty.

At the other end of things, a standard 28-gauge skeet load of No. 9s holds 439 pellets. This makes for splendidly dense patterns, but No. 9s are themselves severely limited when it comes to game shooting. They're adequate for quail over dogs, woodcock, doves close in, and sometimes even for ruffed grouse, but that's about it. To my thinking, 9s are just too light, too bereft of energy to be useful as a versatile game load, regardless of gauge.

My favorite 28-gauge load is a charge of No. 8. I've shot a lot of birds with No. 7½, but there are more than 40 additional No. 8 pellets in a ¾ ounce charge, which improves pattern density, and their energy capacity is only slightly less.

So it's a compromise, a balancing act in search of the most practical relationship between the number of pellets you have to work with and the amount of energy each pellet can contribute in doing its work for you. Size matters, and yet size is a sword that cuts both ways. But seen from the right perspective, this may be the most compelling argument of all in favor of owning a variety of guns. As every gauge involves some level of compromise, it stands to reason that the only means of being properly prepared for the whole spectrum of shooting is to have at least one of each . . . . Works for me.

NOMINAL PELLET COUNT PER STANDARD CHARGE, IN OUNCES

	1½	1⅜	1¼	1⅛	1	⅞	¾	½
No. 4	202	185	169	152	135	118	102	67
No. 5	255	234	213	192	170	149	128	85
No. 6	337	309	281	253	225	197	169	112
No. 7	525	481	437	393	350	306	262	175
No. 8	615	564	513	462	410	359	308	205
No. 9	877	804	731	658	585	512	439	292

13

OPTIMAL
LOADS

$\mathbf{F}$or every bore size, there is an optimal shot charge, one that creates the most efficient ballistics. The key rests in the relationship between the shot-column's length and its diameter.

The standard 12-bore game load is 1⅛ ounces, in 16-bore it's one ounce, ⅞-ounce for the 20, and ¾-ounce for the 28. Unless a gun is made specifically for heavier charges, these are the loads for which the barrels are proofed.

In practical terms, this means that a 1⅛ ounce shot charge should perform at optimal efficiency in a bore .329-inch in diameter, just as a ¾ ounce charge is ideal for a .550-inch bore.

Pellets inside a cartridge are stacked in a column of a certain diameter and a certain length, and the more nearly similar the two, the better the exterior ballistics will be. The length is nearly always greater than the diameter, but it shouldn't be greater by much. A load of this sort is often described as "square"; it's something of a misnomer, but the concept is correct.

When a shot charge leaves the muzzle it forms neither a flat, pancake-shaped profile nor a perfectly expanding, straight-walled cone. Instead, according to the best research done thus far, the swarm expands in a bell shape that grows progressively wider with distance. It also has length, usually described as "stringing," with the pellets that were at the bottom of the charge inside the cartridge following behind those at the top.

In the old days, before progressive-burning powders and shot protectors, the string of a 12-bore charge might have been as much as 15 to 20 feet long. What a long string does is open huge gaps in the pattern's profile—large enough, if the timing is right, for a bird to fly straight through the swarm and come out unscathed. Stringing is a phenomenon that doesn't show up on a patterning plate; the plate shows only width and density, not the third dimension of length, which amounts to the time lapse between the first and last pellets to strike.

(Actually, a couple of chaps at the University of London some years ago designed and built a plate that did record elapsed time, but equipment that sophisticated is not available to the average shooter.)

Much of the work in cartridge development over the past 60-odd years has been directed toward shortening shot strings, and has met with excellent success. Now, using first-rate cartridges, the string may be no more than six or eight feet long—provided the load is optimal for the gun.

Obviously, the only way to pack more shot into any cartridge is to lengthen the shot column, and the longer the column inside the shell, the longer the string once it leaves the muzzle. Overloading defeats the cartridge-maker's efforts. Unfortunately, overloading is all too common, especially in the U.S., where the dictum for ammunition has long been: If Some is Good, More Must be Better. In fact, more is often much worse. Case in point, the 3-inch 20-bore. Stuffing 1¼ ounces of shot down a .615-inch diameter barrel accomplishes nothing but dreadful ballistics and vicious recoil.

Sensitivity to overloading increases as the bore grows smaller. The wonderfully versatile 12-bore will shoot anything from 1⅜ to one ounce and do it beautifully. At the other end of the spectrum, nothing can improve upon the 28-bore's ¾ ounce charge. Not that manufacturers haven't tried; years ago, Federal Cartridge brought out a 2⅞-inch 28-gauge shell loaded with about ⅞ ounce of shot. The market was decidedly underwhelmed, and the load soon disappeared. Winchester developed, and still makes, a so-called

28-gauge Magnum—a full ounce of shot in a 2¾-inch case. It is, in a word, awful. Even in my 28s, all of which weigh exactly six pounds, those miserable things give me a headache after about ten shots.

If overloading is the path to disaster, underloading can produce remarkable results. A ⅞ ounce charge in a 12-bore is splendid, as is ¾ ounce in a 20. Recoil is very soft, and the killing power is astonishing. This is true for the same reason that the ¾ ounce 28-gauge is such a deadly little thing: You may be dealing with fewer pellets, but the ultra-short string allows them all to arrive on the target at virtually the same time. And that, I submit, is truly useful ballistics.

(14)

CHAMBERS

$\mathbf{A}$ lot of states define them as "primitive weapons" for the purpose of game laws, but muzzleloading rifles and guns aren't exactly the dinosaurs we sometimes think them to be. True, black powder is dirty-burning, smoky stuff, and it goes off with a percussive crack that soon leaves me with a headache despite the best hearing protection there is. And true, a modern breechloader's locktime and ignition time are faster than those of a flint- or caplock. But it's also true that the muzzleloader in its perfected form was far more ballistically efficient than any of the early breechloaders—and in fact, it took quite a few years before cartridge breechloaders could even come close to achieving the same accuracy and consistency.

I make the distinction of "cartridge" breechloaders because breechloading arms were well known and widely built in England during the mid-18th century, and then went out of fashion for all of a hundred years. And when they finally came back, it wasn't the breechloading concept itself that caused the problem, but rather the cartridge.

Consider. When you're loading powder and loose shot, or bullet or

SHOTGUNS & SHOOTING THREE

ball, from the front end of a barrel and priming from the other, getting a good load is no great trick. All you need is an oversized bullet, a patched ball, or some sort of wadding, and you've got a tight seal that keeps gas from the burning powder behind the projectile, which obviously is where you want it to be.

Trying to achieve the same thing with a self-contained, cased cartridge isn't so easy, and shot cartridges proved most difficult of all.

First, unlike a rifle cartridge, in which the bullet can protrude and line up perfectly with the lede of the barrel, everything in a shotshell has to be sealed inside the case. A bullet is also its own gas seal, but a shot charge isn't, so there has to be something inside the case, behind the shot column, that's capable of sealing the bore—and it has to be expandable in order to accommodate variations in bore size up to several thousandths of an inch.

Fortunately, cartridge makers found a fairly simple solution to this by using felt or fiber wads. But the cartridge itself posed a considerably thornier problem for gunmakers.

Because ballistic efficiency depends so heavily upon the gas seal in the bore, the inside diameter of the cartridge case needs to be the same, or nearly the same, as the inside diameter of the barrel. But the barrel also has to accommodate the outside diameter of the case, and that varies according to the thickness of the case wall. This may be quite thin, as in a brass or zinc case, relatively thick as in a wound-paper case, or somewhere in between as in a modern plastic case—but a breechloader has to have a chamber of some sort.

The exceptions are guns bored specifically for metal-cased shells. These are typically called "chamberless," although it's a misnomer because most were slightly overbored at the breech, and in any event, very few guns were made that way. From the beginning, wound-paper cases were easier and cheaper to produce and therefore became the standard.

This in turn meant that gunmakers had to establish certain standards. A muzzleloader's bore can be any size the barrelmaker wants it to be; all he has to do is supply a wad-cutter of the same diameter, and the shooter is home free. And even a cutter isn't absolutely necessary, because you can effectively wad a muzzleloader with crumpled-up paper, cloth, leather, grass, almost anything that'll hold together well enough to form a seal.

Self-contained cartridges changed all that. With standardized shell cases came the need for standardized barrel diameters—particularly chamber diameters. Expandable, and compressible, wadding offers some latitude in how large or small a bore can be and still perform efficiently, but chambers aren't nearly so forgiving. A chamber that's even marginally too small simply won't accept a cartridge, and one that's more than marginally too large allows a case to split open and gas to escape past the wadding and shot, which wrecks ballistic efficiency and in some instances can wreck the barrel itself, to say nothing of the shooter.

The English Gun Barrel Proof Act of 1868 established standard bore measurements for no fewer than 63 gauges, from A gauge at two inches in diameter, down to 50-bore at .453-inch. For muzzleloaders, they were all equally practical. Cartridge makers, however, were quick to see that manufacturing shell cases in 63 different sizes was not the most economical course, so they began to standardize cartridges according to size intervals that covered shooters' needs without leaving any practical gaps in performance. Chemistry, in the form of better propellants, eventually rendered the 4-, 8-, and 10-bores obsolete, and good sense convinced shooters that anything smaller than 32-gauge was woefully inefficient. Even the 32 ultimately faded away in the face of the infinitely better 28-gauge—and don't even get me started on the .410.

My point here is that modern shotgun gauges came to be standard because of chambers rather than bores. Gunmakers learned that chambers of a certain size could accommodate bores over a certain range of sizes—as many as three or even four "gauges" in diameter. So, a "12-gauge" gun can have a bore diameter as small as .710-inch (13-gauge) or as large as .740-inch, which is approaching 11-gauge. We call it "12-gauge" because its chamber will accept a standard 12-gauge cartridge.

Among English guns, the distinctions are expressed in the proof marks. Contrary to popular belief, the device of "12" over "c" inside a diamond does not signify a 12-gauge with choke-bored barrels; it stands for "12-gauge chamber." The bore itself is expressed as "12" over "1" (.740-inch), "12" (.729-inch), "13" over "1" (.719-inch), or "13" (.710-inch).

Similar ranges apply to the other gauges as well. A gun that's nominally 20-gauge—that is, has a 20-gauge chamber—can have a bore anywhere in diameter from 19-gauge (.626-inch) to 22-gauge (.596-inch).

Not surprisingly, it took some time for gun and cartridge makers to work all this out so that everyone was singing off the same page. And while that was happening, gunmakers had yet another problem to solve—one that hasn't been fully resolved even yet.

If a gun barrel is a certain size and its chamber a certain degree larger, there has to be a transition between the two. It's called the forcing cone, a section where the chamber diameter tapers down to bore diameter. It may be as short as a half-inch or less, as long as an inch or more.

Current fashion favors long, gradually tapering cones on the notion that the less abrupt transition reduces felt recoil as the shot charge makes its way from case to bore. Pure recoil is an immutable, computable physical reaction of a gun to its ammunition, and the shape of the forcing cone doesn't change that. But kick, which is our perception of recoil, is influenced by all sorts of things, and I'm inclined to agree that longer cones soften the sensation a bit.

More objectively, longer cones appear to improve patterns as well. When a shot column slams against an abrupt constriction, even pellets that are protected by a polyethylene collar are sure to suffer some deformation, and deformed pellets are useless. Not everyone agrees that long cones have any appreciable effect, but the experiments I've done suggest that they promote slightly denser patterns.

What's not open to question is that forcing cones can play mischief with breech pressure when you fire a cartridge that is substantially longer— a quarter-inch or more—than the chamber. In the proper relationship, a chamber is the same length as the cartridge case in its fully open, fired state. When a case is too long, its mouth opens into the forcing cone rather than into the chamber, which means it can't open completely, which in turn means the shot charge and wad are squeezed through an opening smaller than their diameter. The result is a pressure spike—less severe and of shorter duration with a thin-mouthed plastic case and a slick polyethylene wad than with a paper case and fiber wad, but there's a spike nonetheless.

Not shooting long shells in short chambers is universal wisdom, but there also is evidence to suggest that under certain circumstances, shooting short shells in long chambers may be even worse. When the shot charge has to make a jump of a half-inch or more between the case and the forcing cone, the wad may become a momentarily ineffective seal. Wads, remember, are designed to seal bores, not chambers, and those with short obturating skirts may allow a substantial amount of gas to blow past the shot while the column is still in the chamber. At best, this impairs the efficiency of the pattern; at worst, it can upset the wad and make it the equivalent of a barrel obstruction when it reaches the forcing cone.

This is not to say you're courting disaster by shooting 2¾-inch cartridges in three-inch chambers. In all the instances I know of where barrel ruptures are attributable to upset wads, there's been at least a half-inch difference between the length of the case and the chamber. And a blowout isn't necessarily inevitable even where that much difference exists. It all seems to depend on the design of the wad and its ability to expand in the chamber.

As the bottom line, however, I'd recommend adopting the policy of not using cartridges that are more than a quarter-inch shorter than the chambers of your gun. Even though the risk may be minimal, this is an instance where the trouble of being safe is more than justified by the potential for being sorry.

In some ways, modern guns are to muzzleloaders what current automobiles are to those we had years ago. I wouldn't trade my Explorer for the 1960 Ford Falcon I drove in college, but at times I look back fondly on the fact that I could usually keep the old beater running with a crescent wrench and some baling wire. Enhanced performance, efficiency, and convenience do not come without a price. A section of gun barrel large enough and long enough to hold a cartridge seems such a simple thing—and in fact, it is. The implications are where things start to get complicated.

15

The Long and Short of Barrels

Short barrels became a shotgunning fad after World War II. For the next 40 years, the gun industry and the sporting press touted barrels of 26 inches or less as the greatest thing since canned beer—faster-handling, less likely to snag in heavy cover and, in a word, "best" for everything but wildfowl and trapshooting.

Since the 1980s, when sporting clays first became popular, the trend has been toward longer barrels—28, 30, and even 32 inches.

Some of the claims made for short barrels were partly true, others not true at all, and declaring any length "best" for all shooters is simply nonsense. Short-barreled guns are quick to start, but just as quick to slow or stop altogether. Slow your swing and you'll miss behind; stop the gun and you'll miss way behind. This is especially critical on crossing shots, like those we often get at doves and ducks.

Moreover, too much gun speed is more often a hindrance than a help, particularly for the shallow, quartering angles so common in upland hunting. For those, you're far better off to make haste slowly.

Those who'd argue that short barrels are less likely to hang up in thick cover probably haven't spent much time in the brush. Every grouse, woodcock, and quail hunter gets his gun tangled now and then, but it's seldom just the muzzle that snags. In cover so thick that you'd have trouble swinging a snub-nosed revolver from the hip, the virtues of short barrels are more theoretical than real.

With modern ammunition, barrel length has no significant practical effect on ballistics, but it can have a profound effect on gun handling. Short-nosed guns tend to be muzzle-light, which makes them whippy and hard to control. Longer barrels usually mean a bit more weight out front, so the gun swings more smoothly and generates more inertia that helps keep the muzzles moving. If that makes it a wee bit slower to start, so what? A successful shot is determined by what's happening when you pull the trigger, not by how fast you got the gun moving in the first place.

Women, youngsters, and small men can get along just fine with short barrels and often find that longer ones feel awkward. For men of average size and larger, the opposite is true. I can't say what's best for you, but I'm about average size—six feet, 175 pounds. All of my game guns have 29- or 30-inch barrels and are balanced so that slightly more than half the total weight is in my leading hand. I use them everywhere, from the prairie to the thickest grouse coverts, and they work just as well either place and in between.

In the end, the gun needs to suit the shooter, not the habitat, because the shooter is the only true measure of what's best.

16

THE SECOND-MOST
INTERESTING RIB

Joseph Manton is reputed to be the first gunmaker to install an elevated rib on a double gun. Whether he actually was, I don't know, but he did obtain a patent in September 1806 that in part covers an "elevating rib." Manton guns of the period show this to be a tall, square-cornered metal bar laid between the barrels from breech to muzzles.

It was called an elevating rib because it was meant to overcome the tendency to shoot low. Apparently, it did, or at least a great many shooters thought it did, because by 1807 virtually every game gun built in London sported a raised rib of some sort. Such was the idea's level of acceptance and acclaim that in his 1816 book *The Complete Farrier and British Sportsman*, Richard Lawrence says, "It will be needless to expatiate on elevated ribs, patent breeches, water proof and collision locks, and similar inventions of the present day, it being evident that gun barrels of different constructions carry with various degrees of truth and efficacy."

Although the last part of Mr. Lawrence's sentence is a bit murky, the

---

first part certainly isn't, and his comment is notable for two reasons. One is that some sort of rib clearly had become a standard component of the gun by 1815. The other is that Mr. Lawrence possibly was the last gun writer in history who wasn't moved to expound upon all the virtues and intricacies of the shotgun rib.

Fact is, the only other rib that's caused as much controversy, consternation, and sheer confusion is the one reportedly borrowed from Adam some time back.

The matter hasn't always been as complicated as it is now. Throughout the 19th century and the 20th, there were only two basic types, game ribs and pigeon ribs, and while both allowed for some variation, the typical double-gun rib was essentially either one or the other.

Not surprisingly, the game rib developed along with the English game gun, a trim, lightweight piece designed for driven birds and rough shooting, a gun, in which balance, dynamics, and other handling qualities are of paramount importance. We'd call it a "bird gun," tailored to respond quickly and smoothly in field shooting situations.

For a variety of reasons, most of which have to do with weight, balance, and the way the gun is meant to be used, the game rib lies low between the barrels. In one form, it curves with the taper of the barrels; this is called a swamped rib. In another, its profile is a straight line from breech to muzzle and is therefore called a straight rib. The cross section may be hollow or flat, that is, concave or level across the top.

The best way to keep them all squared up is to remember that "swamped" and "straight" refer to how a rib is shaped from end to end, while "hollow" and "flat" describe its shape from side to side.

Although a game rib technically can be made in any combination of these forms, most are either swamped and hollow or straight and flat. Hollow ribs typically are polished and blacked, while flat ones usually are stippled or cross hatched or finished in some other way that creates a non-reflective, matte surface. The swamped, hollow version still is the classic British and European form; for reasons I'll get to presently, American gunmakers have largely preferred straight, flat ribs.

In contrast to the light and lively game gun, the pigeon gun is relatively heavy and long barreled, just like a modern-day trap gun. In fact, it's the original trap gun, meant to be used on pigeons sprung from boxlike traps.

It was designed to achieve the optimum in deliberate, precise pointing over a fairly short swing.

The old-time pigeon rib is usually straight and flat, but it's noticeably wider and taller than a game rib. It typically stands well above the barrels through most of its length and is almost always matte finished. A lot of pigeon ribs also show a distinct taper from breech to muzzle.

Between them, these two represented about all there was in shotgun ribs for a hundred years, and indeed, they still represent opposite functions. The practical difference between a pigeon rib and a swamped, hollow game rib is that one is meant to be clearly seen by the shooter and the other isn't.

Even in the days of Joe Manton and the first James Purdey, pigeon shooting was as highly formalized as trap shooting is today. The shooter is allowed to stand at a predetermined place and shoulder his gun before he calls for the target. The target itself is small and, in the case of clay target trap, always presents a going-away shot within a fairly narrow range of angles. This puts a premium on very precise pointing. All told, the game of trap is about the nearest thing to rifle shooting that can be done with a shotgun and a moving target.

In this, a bold, eye-catching rib is an asset. It offers a good reference as you mount the gun, settle it against your shoulder and cheek, and adjust the position of your head to get your master eye precisely aligned with the barrel. Once that's accomplished, you extend your focus out to where the target will be, and you're ready to shoot. In sum, an obvious rib is every bit as useful as sights on a rifle, and for exactly the same reasons.

The game rib is not meant to be a strong attraction to the eye. It isn't supposed to stand out sharply from the barrels, only to act as a subtle reference in a shooter's peripheral vision, allowing him to keep his attention fully on whatever it is he's trying to shoot. Clay targets are predictable, and so to some extent are box-bird pigeons. Game birds are not. Even with the help of a pointing dog, a hunter has only a vague idea of where the birds will appear and an even vaguer notion of what angle their flight lines will take. The more attention you can give to the target, and the less you have to give to the gun, the more successful you're likely to be.

This presupposes two conditions: Your gun should fit properly, and your technique should be such that you mount it the same way every time. If the gun fits and you handle it consistently, you don't need a strong visual reference from the rib. It will simply point where you're looking.

I said earlier that the American gun trade most often used straight, flat ribs. Even those makers who put in a bit of swamp or hollow didn't use much, and you'll look a very long time to find an American rib that isn't matted. The effect isn't quite as eye riveting as a pigeon or target rib, but it claims more attention than a traditional English game rib.

The reason is that American guns were made to factory specifications rather than the customers'. In that case, a more obvious rib is a distinct advantage, because it allows the shooter to fit himself to the gun each time he shoots it. If you can see the rib, then you have a reference point for getting your eye aligned with the barrels. It certainly is not the ideal, but it's better than nothing.

Quite a few people have told me they don't shoot well with a traditional game rib. Invariably, it's been with guns that didn't fit in the first place, so that's not surprising. Spend a lifetime adapting yourself to a variety of guns, and you're naturally going to develop a set of unconscious habits, one of which is to always look for the rib. The harder it is to find, the more of your attention it takes away from the target.

So if the gun fits perfectly and your technique is perfectly consistent, why do you need a rib at all? Under those circumstances, you don't, really. But I have yet to meet a game shot so accomplished that he didn't benefit from a bit of help now and then, and for the rest of us, it's more often now than then.

Besides, guiding the eye is not the rib's only function. Remember Manton's elevating rib? What he was trying to elevate wasn't the rib itself but rather the shot swarm. Depending upon how it's designed, a rib can make a gun shoot higher or lower (also to one side or the other, but if it does that, the barrelmaker screwed up), and of the two, higher is by far more useful.

Raising the shot-swarm's point of impact in relation to the shooter's line of sight offers several advantages. For one thing, you don't have to blot out a rising or incoming bird if your gun shoots a wee bit high. The old rule of thumb on shooting driven grouse, for instance, is to shoot at their feet as they're coming toward you, for the game gun traditionally is designed to place about three-fifths of its shot charge above the line of sight. The same arrangement works equally well on rising quail or woodcock or pheasants; it allows you to keep the bird in sight as your muzzles converge with it, but doesn't shoot so high that you have to float the target above the barrels and thereby lose contact with its flight line.

Getting this right for every shooter is one element of what well-fitted guns are all about, and it's accomplished in part by the height of the stock comb and in part by the rib. If the rear end of the rib is higher above the centerline of the bore than the front end is, holding the rib level naturally elevates the muzzle. So, when the stockmaker gets the dimensions to the point where you're looking right down the rib when the comb touches your cheek, the rib pitch ensures that the proper elevation falls into place. When the entire rib is the same height above the bore centers, as it is in some single-barrel and over/under guns, any adjustment of elevation belongs solely with the stock.

As the clay target replaced live pigeons in trap shooting around the turn of the 20th century, the whole matter of shotgun ribs became more complex. So far as I know, the Baker single barrel, announced to the market in 1909, was the first American gun to be fitted with a ventilated rib. (Actually, fitted is the wrong word; in about the first 300 guns, the rib was integral with the barrel, a milling operation that must have been horrendously expensive even by the standards of the day.)

At any rate, the ventilated rib caught on immediately. By 1920 it was standard fare among single shots and repeaters, eventually achieved the same status for over/unders, and often was applied to side-by-side doubles as well. Apart from being somewhat lighter weight than a solid rib, the vent rib's prime virtue is that it allows heat from the barrel to dissipate more readily while at the same time keeping the mirage effect to a minimum. Without a rib, the shimmer of heat waves can play hob with your ability to see the target in sharp focus.

As target guns became more and more specialized, ribs naturally came in for a share of high-tech treatment, beginning with Browning's Broadway. Some trap shooters liked the Broadway rib; personally, I always found its extreme width extremely distracting.

Very high ribs, anywhere from a half inch to an inch or more, enjoy a certain vogue among target shooters. They look weird, for sure, but they do have some practical use. With a high rib and a high-combed stock, you can mount the gun quite low on your shoulder and thereby noticeably reduce the effects of recoil. My favorite piece for skeet and sporting clays is a

Marocchi Contrast with a half-inch-tall rib, and though it perennially jars my sense of how guns ought to look, it's the most comfortable target gun I've ever shot.

A few makers, notably Browning, have designed target ribs that can be adjusted for pitch, which is not at all a bad way to refine a factor-gun's point of impact. More recently still, the rising popularity of sporting clays has brought about some new rib designs: high, low, tapered, and the like. For some reason a lot of makers have settled on 13mm as a sort of standard width for clays-gun ribs. Having shot quite a few of these, I can't honestly say I notice they offer any advantage over a narrower rib, but on the other hand, they aren't wide enough to bother me, either.

These and similar developments have been confined almost exclusively to single barrels and over/unders. Very few significant improvements of any kind have been wrought upon the side-by-side in this century. The only exception where ribs are concerned is the one Robert Churchill designed, though I've never been entirely convinced that it's as significant as some gun scholars seem to think. The Churchill rib is a double-tapered affair. In cross-section it looks like a flat-topped pyramid, and depending on the gauge of the gun, it might be less than an eighth-inch wide at the muzzles. Functionally, it's meant to create an optical illusion.

Churchill was a great advocate of 25-inch barrels, and he designed his tapered rib to give a shooter the illusion of longer tubes. Actually, a Churchill rib works perfectly well as a guide to the eye; it's unobtrusive and it really does make you think you're looking down a longer set of barrels. But what that could possibly do to make any difference in handling, I haven't a clue. The important thing is how a gun is balanced, how it feels, not how it looks. No amount of optical foolery is going to make a whippy, muzzle-light gun feel like anything else.

Very short barrels are fine for those who can truly handle them, and I have no quarrel with Mr. Churchill's rib, but to call them revolutionary, or even a minimal improvement, is hogwash.

But then so are a lot of things touted to be the next great thing or the new great age of guns and gunning. And that's okay. No manufacturer, whether of guns, automobiles, or widgets, is likely to get far with a marketing approach that simply says, "This is new but not really better; it's just different." It's up to us, and history, to decide what's really significant and what isn't, wherein resides the fun of it. This would be a dull business without a generous quotient of hogwash. I have a notion Joe Manton knew that perfectly well, because a lot of his "inventions" were frivolous nonsense. But I'll bet he had no idea what a can of worms he was opening when he came up with his elevating rib.

(17)

Ejectors

Acquiring your first side-by-side gun can be about as bewildering as marrying your first wife, except that with the gun the bafflement usually comes before you get it, rather than afterward.

I know this because it's a rare month when I don't receive a dozen or more letters from first-timers asking for advice. About guns, I mean; I'm not exactly ill-qualified to comment on the other, but I'm more comfortable offering advice on something I truly do understand.

The problem is that guns require certain choices in physical makeup, while wives tend to come with all accessories included. A gun can be fully serviceable in its most basic form—barrels, an action, a stock, lockwork, and a trigger. Beyond that, you're into the realm of choices: What gauge; how long should the barrels be; should the chokes be screw-ins or fixed, and if fixed, how much constriction; what stock configuration and dimensions will work best; should it have one trigger or two; ejectors or extractors; this or that, on and on.

The answers to most of these lie in the buyer's expectations and in the purpose he intends the gun to fulfill. If he tells me he's looking for a grouse

---

gun, I can pretty well rule out suggesting an eight-pound 12-bore, and if he's a goose hunter, I won't be recommending a 28-gauge.

But some choices have less to do with purpose than with function and efficiency. I usually advise against single triggers for side-by-sides, regardless of whether it's to be a quail gun or a wildfowler. There are some good single triggers available, but also a whole lot of others that are apt to be a pain in the butt sooner or later. Double triggers are more reliable, more efficient, more durable, more everything that we want guns to be.

My advice would be the opposite for an over/under, incidentally. For one thing, it's hard to find an over/under that doesn't have a single trigger, and they are generally more reliable than those for side-bys. There are mechanical reasons for this, but now isn't the time to get into them.

The one thing I always recommend is to get a gun with ejectors.

Oftentimes, it's a moot point; except for the bare-bones economy models, virtually all new guns come with ejectors. But those who hanker after an older American piece will find lots of mid- and lower-grade guns that don't have them.

Time was, ejectors were like air conditioners in automobiles—pricy options whose value wasn't necessarily self-evident. American makers typically offered them as standard in the higher grades, but if you wanted them in a lower-grade gun, you had to pay extra, anywhere from $10 to $25, or more. That was serious money at a time when $100 would buy a middle-grade gun brand-new, and a lot of men chose to forego the extra expense. (Though I don't know how they could possibly have resisted the chance to own a gun with "selective automatic ejectors," as the catalogs and ads usually called them. The phrase always makes me smile. Selective, I hope; the system would be pretty useless if live shells and empties alike came flying out every time you opened the gun. And if they weren't "automatic," they wouldn't be "ejectors.")

I certainly wouldn't advise anyone to turn down a good gun at a reasonable price just because it didn't have ejectors, but on the other hand, if it's to be your main bird gun, I would recommend finding one that does have them. You'll pay a bit more, but you'll also get more.

When you're shooting targets, tweezing empties out with your fingers is no problem. It's not a problem when you're hunting, either, if you don't mind losing good opportunities to shoot while you're looking at the gun and fumbling around trying to get hold of the hulls.

The quicker you can get reloaded, the better—whether to give you a crack at the almost-inevitable sleeper in a covey of quail or sharptails or Huns or chickens, the pair of doves that come zipping along right on the tails of the ones you've just fired at, or the rooster whose nerves are a wee bit steadier than his colleague's. It is axiomatic that game birds flush closer, fly slower, and offer far easier shots when your gun is empty.

And the more easily you can get reloaded without having to look away from where the birds might appear, the better able you'll be to take those unexpected shots when they come.

Clearly, a break-action gun cannot be self-loading, but with ejectors it becomes self-unloading, and that's half the battle.

I've heard all the arguments against ejectors, and they're all hogwash, starting with the old wheeze that you don't really need them. Of course you don't, any more than you really need air conditioning or a heater in your car—but I'll bet you have both, because they make driving more comfortable and efficient. Ejectors do the same for shooting.

Ejectors are just one more thing to go wrong. This can be true of systems that are poorly designed or badly made. None of the American ejectors were badly made, but some certainly weren't very good designs. Given enough use, any mechanism can go out of whack, even such wonderfully simple, reliable ones as the Southgate-type systems widely used by English and European makers. As the bottom line, though, any good gunsmith will tell you that ninety percent of the "ejector problems" he sees are the result of "repairs" attempted by bozos who didn't have a clue what they were doing.

I want to save my hulls for reloading, but I can't do that with ejectors. Of course you can. Ejectors give you a choice; you can either let the empties fly or catch them, and it's perfectly simple and easy to do either one.

If you want to keep your hulls, whether you're a reloader or just someone who doesn't want to litter the landscape with cast-off empties, here's how to do it. After firing, rotate the gun a quarter-turn clockwise (if you're right-handed), clamp the stock between your ribs and your elbow, thumb the lever, and as you pull the barrels down, raise your hand and cup it over the breech three or four inches away from the barrels. The ejectors won't trip until the action is nearly at full gape, so you have plenty of time to get your hand in place, even when you're in a hurry. Keeping your hand back from the breech allows the ejectors to kick the hulls clear of the chambers and right into your grasp. With a little practice, you can do it without looking.

When you choose to catch depends on the situation. Shooting doves and driven game, I always let 'em fly. Speed is usually of the essence, and because I'm standing in one place, the empties won't be hard to gather up afterward.

I'll occasionally do the same with flushing birds if I think more flushes are imminent. At those times, the empties aren't always so easy to find, but a little searching usually turns them up.

Most often, though, I catch the empties, drop them into my game-pouch, and pick up fresh ones from my right-hand vest or coat pocket. After so many years, it has become a completely unconscious sequence of catch-back-forward-load. Just recently I watched myself shooting quail on video, filmed from behind, and I was surprised at how quickly I perform that little ritual; I'm scarcely aware of doing it at all, much less doing it fast.

Which goes to show, I guess, that even the coordination-impaired can learn to make an efficient move with only a few hundred-thousand reps of practice. But it wouldn't work without the ejectors.

Some guns, notably the old side-plate Lefevers and the current Berettas, offer means of deactivating the ejectors by turning a screw or moving a switch. Fact is, you can make any gun an extractor-only just by removing the ejector springs. It's a simple job, though best done by a gunsmith if you don't have a spring-cramp.

But I really don't know why anyone would want to disable ejectors. They serve a useful purpose, and if properly adjusted they're as reliable as any other part of a gun. Nowadays, there's just no good reason not to have them.

(18)

Bringing Them Back

Reading the letter brought others like it suddenly into focus. "I shoot a 1926 L.C. Smith Field Grade," the gentleman wrote. "I would like the stock refinished, barrels reblued (and a ding removed), the checkering brought back and the case colors redone. In short, I would like it to look newer. It is not fancy but very sure and dependable. I wonder if you would give me the names of a couple of gunsmiths. I don't need nor can afford an artist."

I've received a lot of letters like this one over the years. They are invariably written from the heart and brim with the best of intentions. Almost as often, they represent what's commonly known as A Can of Worms.

Not because there's anything technically impossible about restoring an old gun, nor because there's anything wrong with the notion of wanting an old gun to look new again. But restoration involves both an emotional aspect and an economic side, and that's where issues that seem clear-cut can grow murky in an instant.

There are essentially three approaches to reworking older guns. Upgrading is a matter of turning a plain factory gun into the cosmetic equivalent of any higher grade in which that particular make was originally offered—having, for instance, a Fox Sterlingworth restocked and engraved to look like an XE Grade, or in the same way turning a Parker VHE into an A-1 Special. The motivation can be as innocent as simply wanting a high-grade version of some favorite gun without taking the trouble of finding an original. Or it can be as devious as turning a plain-Jane into a knockout in order to reap a high selling price by passing it off as original. ("Fraud" and "counterfeit" are other popular terms for this latter sort of thing, and such guns do exist.)

Another approach is to use an older factory gun as the basis for a full custom job, a gun that's custom-stocked, reworked, and decorated specifically to its owner's taste. In the end, it may not look like any factory-made version of the same gun. There's some good economic sense in this; top-quality custom work isn't cheap, but the result can be a custom gun for considerably less money than it takes to have one built from scratch in England or Italy. At least one American gunsmith—Steven Dodd Hughes of Livingston, Montana—has made a specialty of this sort of thing, and has turned out some magnificent pieces.

Restoration can be equally straightforward. Refinish the wood, recut the checkering, reblue the barrels, re-case-harden the frame, perhaps pick up the engraving, and you have an old gun that looks brand-new. Or rather, you *can* have that. You can also have a botched-up mess, or some glossy clone with all the character of a plastic fork. Or a formerly valuable gun with most of its value destroyed. In the collectors' market for old American guns, condition and factory originality are everything; the ideal is one that's exactly as it was when it left the factory and shows no evidence of use. Some use and no alteration represent the next level, and collector desirability diminishes from there in direct proportion to how much a gun's been used and what's been altered.

For the purposes of this discussion, let's assume we're talking about guns with no particular collector's value, guns that have been well used but remain in essentially sound mechanical condition.

On the face of it, restoration can seem a wonderful idea, but when it comes up against the questions *why?*, *how?*, *by whom?*, and *for how much?*, things often get complicated.

Why generally elicits one of two answers: I want it to look handsomer than it does now, or I want it to look newer. To the first, I say amen. Anyone who views guns as something more than mere tools appreciates their intrinsic beauty, and bringing back some of the original glow to a nice old gun pays respect to the craftsmanship and materials that went into it.

You'll notice I said "some" of the original glow. How you approach restoration doesn't necessarily have to mean full-scale cosmetic surgery. The simplest, and in some ways most striking, face-lift you can give a gun is to have the wood refinished; replacing years of accumulated dirt, sweat, and oil with a new, hand-rubbed finish can make an otherwise well-worn gun look lovely. Having the checkering cleaned and pointed-up at the same time only makes it that much better.

Though I'm in favor of giving virtually any old gun a stock job, I am personally seldom inclined to go much farther. I understand that making a gun look brand-new, or virtually so, appeals to some, but I'm not one of them. To me, a new gun can be beautiful, but it lacks character, doesn't communicate any feeling that it's ever been anywhere or done anything. New guns look sterile. But one that shows some honest wear, some sense of having spent time in somebody's hands, of having been out in the weather, crossed a few fences and slugged through some bramble thickets, maybe even been trampled a bit by rowdy pups—now there's a gun that can steal my heart.

Good, honest wear is a legacy passed from one hunter to another. I've owned a lot of guns whose former owners I never knew except through the runes and heiroglyphics that time and use inevitably writes in wood and steel, and unless the dings and scratches made some difference in how well or how safely the guns would function, I've never even thought of removing them. To me it would feel like erasing evidence that someone before me loved what I love.

I've also owned a few guns that belonged to people I did know, which only made my wish to leave them as they were all the stronger. I refinished and recheckered the stocks of my father's old pump gun long ago, when he was still alive, but even then I took care not to take out any scratches or dents, some of which he put there before I was born. It's been more than twenty years since we last followed the dogs together in search of pheasants or quail, and almost as long since he's been gone, but I can still read part of his history, and ours, on his gun.

Now there are instances when more extensive refinishing is truly necessary. Any dents in barrels simply must be repaired if a gun is to be a safe and reliable shooter, and sometimes that calls for rebluing. I've also had ribs come loose on a few old guns, and when a rib's been relayed, rebluing is a must.

Beyond that, rebluing and color-hardening are solely cosmetic, and it's therefore up to the individual to decide whether he wants it done. To some, it's what restoration is all about. That's fine, so long as you know the risks.

Even a moderately skilled amateur can usually refinish wood if he takes his time, is careful not to round off any edges or corners, and goes through all the grits with his sandpaper. But refinishing metal is a job for a professional, and by that I mean a real pro, not just some ham-fisted clod who calls himself a gunsmith and thinks a high-speed buffing wheel is the way to polish a gun. Properly bluing gun steel requires skill, experience, patience, and a well-equipped workshop; color case-hardening requires all that to the nth degree. Just off the top of my head, I could name a dozen or more craftsmen in North America who do superb bluing work, but I know only a couple to whom I'd trust any of my guns for color-hardening.

The line in the letter I quoted at the beginning that sent chills up my back is the one that read, "I don't need nor can afford an artist." I had to tell him that the one thing he really couldn't afford was to have the work he wanted done by anyone but a top-notch craftsman.

One of the world's great truths is that you get what you pay for, and paying a cut-rate price for restoration work all too often means that what you get is a ruined gun. I've seen them, and they're enough to make you sick.

How would you feel, I wrote back to that good chap, if you sent away this nice old gun you love so much and got it back badly polished and poorly blued? And what if someone re-case-hardens it so ineptly that the frame and lockplates are warped to the point that nothing fits together any longer? Is having it look newer worth the risk of having it look awful?

There is no economic sense in paying any price for shoddy work. You're not only out the price of the work, but you've also paid somebody to destroy most of the value of your gun. The old saw about being penny-wise and pound-foolish applies. Bottom line is that if you can't afford best-quality work, don't have it done at all.

I don't know what my correspondent ultimately decided to do. I gave him names of men who could perform the work he wanted, but I hope I also gave him something to think about. When you come right down to it, what I really hope is that I saved him the anguish of seeing a faithful old companion desecrated and helped preserve all the good memories of the places they've been together and the things they've done.

The Arrow
and the Indian

A lot of us are not content to simply own our guns. We want relationships with them, want them to be part of us, want our guns to be extensions of our will, of our sense of beauty and value, our sense of sport, of history.

I suppose it's a guy thing, maybe even a Freudian guy thing. I haven't met many women who wanted a relationship with a mechanical object (and if you're thinking what I think you're thinking, don't go there). Women seem content to let mechanical things remain just that—useful perhaps, but ultimately separate from their psyches. A lot of men, on the other hand, view guns as something more than the sum of their parts—to the extent that we want our guns to represent not only what we do but also who we are. We feel the same way, in fact, about our automobiles, fly rods, golf clubs, pool cues, whatever we use to do the things we love.

I started thinking about this last fall, when a friend and I talked about a gun he'd just bought. "I *really* like it," he said. "I'd like it to become my favorite gun, but I'd also like to shoot it better."

This is not an uncommon sentiment, though I seldom hear it put so succinctly. And it raises the old question of which is more important, the arrow or the Indian.

Everyone who wants a relationship wants it to be ideal. Every Indian wants his perfect arrow, and for every arrow there's a perfect Indian, at least potentially. The trick, of course, is getting the two matched up.

It's a complex process, because we and our guns interrelate in complex ways, beginning with the fact that some guns appeal to us more than others. Exactly why we especially like one gun, or one sort of gun, is as subjective as choosing a wife. It originates in the blood, not in the cranium. It also reveals our individual natures. I'm highly visual, for instance, and could no more make an ugly gun my perfect arrow than I could marry a woman I wasn't pleased to look at every day.

How shallow, some might say, but I don't think so. I have a powerful sense of physical beauty, so why deny it? Beauty may be only skin deep, but ugly goes clear to the bone. That the gun, or the woman, I find unutterably lovely may not appeal to the next guy only underscores the fact that we're all different. The point is that for any gun to become your perfect arrow, you first have to *like* it, *really* like it.

But there's more. Having, finally, learned that there's a difference between beauty and substance, appearance is only the starting point. I want a gun that's pleasing to my eyes, but it also has to have sound barrels, good balance, crisp triggers, reliable ejectors, and everything else that assures me it'll go *bang* when I want it to and that the shot will go where I look.

There also are different kinds of substance. My friend put it this way: "I wanted a British Best because I wanted to hunt with a gun that is as fine as could be made by the hand of man, a gun someone put his heart and soul into, one with some history that perhaps I can add to, and one that I can pass on to be held and touched and dreamed over."

Well said. For a lot of us, our guns represent a tangible link to the traditions of our sport, traditions we delight in preserving, traditions we hope to pass on to those who come after us.

A romantic notion, certainly, but what of that? I know some die-hard shooters who don't care a hoot for romance, who cherish their guns for the engineering and craftsmanship that goes into them; I know some others who are perfectly happy with just about any old clunk simply because it stands for the heritage of our sport; and I know yet others who take keen delight in how their guns appeal to both their heads and hearts.

Who's right? All of them. Your perfect arrow begins with whatever you find most appealing, for whatever reason. You don't have to be able to explain why—you don't even have to know why. You just have to like it, at levels where rationality does not apply.

But there's a catch. You may think some gun is your perfect arrow, but that doesn't mean you're its perfect Indian. It's not a matter of either side being at fault, but rather of incompatibility. Fact is, an ideal relationship cannot be one-sided.

I learned this the hard way, about thirty years ago, when I fell in love with a little Parker 16-gauge that I thought was the be-all and end-all of guns. I loved everything about it, from the length of its barrels to the dog's-head logo on the buttplate to the mere fact that it was a Parker. Unfortunately, it loved nothing about me. It was too short at both ends, balanced all wrong for the way I shoot, choked too tightly for the hunting I did, and was stocked for someone with a physique very different from mine. We spent three utterly miserable years together before I had to admit that this was an arrow that needed some other Indian. I sold it with a distinct feeling of relief and promised myself that I would never again be so blind.

And I haven't been, for the most part. With only occasional lapses, I've kept sight of the fact that my guns need to fulfill certain basic requirements if we're to be happy together. They need to meet some standards of weight and length, balance and dimension, function and form, and any that don't are not candidates for a match made in heaven.

There is a sound analogy here between guns and spouses. You can fall hopelessly in love with a pretty face, but unless there is a distinct commonality of values, beliefs, temperament, goals, and outlook, you simply cannot shovel enough love into the relationship to make it work. I know this; I've tried it.

Same with guns. Unless you choose realistically, you're choosing wrongly. A five-pound 28-bore that feels like a toothpick in your hands may be the most adorable thing you've ever seen, but if you're six-foot-two and can juggle bowling balls, it isn't ever going to be your best gun. Similarly, if you're five-six and slightly built, you're never going to shoot well with a long-nosed, nine-pound magnum, no matter how much you love it.

Even when you do choose realistically, a perfect relationship is by no means a foregone conclusion. You and your bride may be precisely of a mind on every fundamental issue in life, your personalities may be complementary, and you may be zeroed in on exactly the same objectives in life, but you still have to adapt to one another. It may be tragic that Romeo and Juliet died young and for no good reason, but at least they don't have to deal with different sleeping schedules, snoring, differing habits of leaving lights off or on in unoccupied rooms, personal tolerances for how warm or cool a house ought to be, or any of the hundred other little things that require mutual adaptation, tolerance, and compromise.

And here, too, it's the same with guns. If your relationship is going to be ideal, you and your gun are probably both going to have to change a bit. How much depends upon how wisely you've chosen in the first place. You can't turn a four-pound 28-bore into a seven-pound 12-gauge, nor vice versa, but you can turn a gun that's almost right into one that's exactly right. If you start with one that basically suits you, getting the rest of the way is only a matter of refinement.

Barrel length and overall weight are the key considerations in finding what basically suits you. Both strongly influence handling characteristics, and the first thing you need to find is a gun that you'll be able to carry, swing, and mount with optimal efficiency. You want one that's neither too heavy nor too light for your size and upper-body strength, and one with barrels neither too long nor too short for your height and the length of your arms. For men of average height, build, and strength, this usually means a gun, regardless of gauge, that weighs somewhere between six and seven pounds and has barrels no less than 28 inches long—but in any event, what's most important is that no gun can become your perfect arrow if its weight and barrel length don't suit you.

Never, ever, choose a gun solely because of the stock. Your potential arrow may be dressed in the most gorgeous piece of walnut that ever grew, and the stock may fit you to a gnat's whisker, but if that's the *only* thing about it that's right, it'll never be your perfect gun. Of the main components of a gun, stocks are the easiest, and cheapest, to alter or replace.

Chances are, the path to your perfect arrow is going to involve some stock work and maybe some metal work as well. You might need to have the triggers tuned or the chokes altered to deliver optimal patterns for the type of shooting you do. The more nearly right the gun is to begin with, the less you'll need to have done to make it exactly right. But whatever it needs, do it.

We Americans have an ingrained reluctance to alter guns, and the sooner we get over that, the happier we'll be. It derives from collecting, from the axiom that the more a gun has been altered from factory-original condition, the less valuable it is. This is true—of collector's guns. But we're not talking about collector's guns here; we're talking about guns to shoot. The fact is, most older guns that have seen much use are not collector's items, regardless of what you've been told. If you have one that truly is, sell it to a collector and buy one that isn't. The chances of achieving your perfect arrow without some kind of alteration are about as slim as finding a poacher's conscience, so don't sabotage yourself. If you want a gun to shoot, do whatever is necessary to make it shootable.

Having a perfect arrow is only half the equation. You have to become your arrow's perfect Indian, and you do that by becoming the best shot you can be. Take a shooting lesson, or several, and learn a sound technique. Set up a regimen for good practice, both at home and on a shooting range, and stick to it. Be diligent, be faithful. Put some real effort into being a better shot, and you will be rewarded.

This of course is the hard part, especially in our age of instant gratification, but there's no other way. A gun can't shoot itself, no matter how perfectly it fits or functions. We've all known guys who are forever tinkering with their guns, changing this, changing that, making minuscule adjustments to their stocks or their chokes or their triggers, ad nauseam. A few, truly expert, are trying to achieve the greatest possible refinement, but more often such incessant fiddling is in fact an attempt to buy a substitute for skill or practice, an attempt to fix something other than what's really broken.

An ideal relationship doesn't just happen. It evolves through thought and effort and attention. It is both a goal and a process. So which is more important, the arrow or the Indian? The question can prompt all manner of interesting discussion and debate, but in the end, the only real answer is: yes.

20

A FULL QUIVER

Not long after I wrote the previous chapter, I was talking with a friend about the arrow-Indian relationship, and after I wound up a précis of what I'd written, he thought for a moment and said, "Then does this imply that a shooter should use just one gun? Or at least identical guns, if he has more than one?"

Which made me think for quite a few moments, for several weeks, in fact. At first glance, that does indeed seem to be the implication, though not the one I intended when I wrote the piece. But it's a valid question: If the perfect arrow-Indian relationship is possible, can there be more than one perfect arrow for each Indian?

Beware the man who shoots one gun is an established axiom in the shooting world. Or as my old friend Aaron Pass once remarked in his inimitable Georgia style, "Never bet money in a quail shoot against a guy carrying a 20-gauge Model 12 that has no bluing or front sight."

I can go along with this, with one provision: beware the man who shoots a lot with just one gun. It's the same wisdom that says don't bet money in a golf match with a guy who has a weird swing—because if he's willing to bet, you can be sure he's found a way to make it work. Just ask the people who bet with Lee Trevino in his young-hustler days.

The one-arrow Indian can be a wicked good shot, but that doesn't necessarily mean he's shooting his perfect arrow. More often it means that he's accommodated himself to the gun and practiced enough that his accommodations are second nature. We are physically adaptable animals, and if we put enough work into it, we can adapt ourselves to just about any gun. It may be too light, too heavy, misbalanced, and not fit worth a damn, but we can still learn to shoot it competently, through dint of sheer effort and perseverance.

But he who does so must perforce become a one-arrow Indian. Give him a different gun, even one that is his perfect arrow, and he has to relearn a whole new set of accommodations. Perfect arrows can't deliver their greatest benefits until we become perfect Indians.

Aha, you might say (if you're inclined to say things like "aha" instead of "bullll...."): If I have to relearn anyway, why go to the bother of finding an optimal gun? Why not just stick with what I have and make it work?

You can if you want, but it seems to me that the one-arrow Indian is missing out on one of the keenest pleasures in gunning—which is to shoot well with more than one gun. And the only way to accomplish that is to make sure that all your guns are optimal, to have a whole quiver full of perfect arrows.

Moreover, they don't have to be identical. They only have to fulfill certain requirements that make them ideally suited to you.

The stocks have to fit; that much is absolute. Every one of your guns has to point right where you look when all you do is lift it to your cheek without moving your head.

They should also have very similar dynamics—which is to say they should each be balanced so that all of them feel much the same in your hands. This will require some tinkering, because even if they all have barrels of the same length, barrel weight and stock weight are apt to be different, but the results are well worth the trouble.

They should also be of similar overall weight. If you're a target shooter as well as a bird hunter, you might want to distinguish between your target guns and game guns and establish two basic weight categories, one for each type.

You want all your trigger-pulls to be similar, too—not necessarily exactly the same weight, because that needs to vary a bit according to the weight of the gun, but they should all feel equally crisp and clean, without any creep or drag.

Beyond that, your various guns may be quite different from one another and still suit you equally well. Or they may be basically alike. The way it's evolved with me, my target guns are 8- to 8¼ pound 12-bore over/unders and my game guns are all side-by-sides.

To use my own little battery as an example, the game guns comprise a John Wilkes 12-bore, an AyA 12, a Fox 20 (one of the new ones), and an Arrieta 28. The stock dimensions are all the same. They all have 29-inch barrels except the Fox, which is 30 inches. The lightest weighs six pounds, the heaviest 6½. They're all balanced to put slightly more than half the weight in my leading hand, and the trigger-pulls are virtually identical.

They are, in short, my perfect arrows, and on the odd occasions when I am their perfect Indian we do okay together.

Given their similarities, you'd think switching from one to another would be a seamless transition. It usually is, but as I learned this winter, there can be some surprising facets to the relationship.

I shot the 28-bore all through November, took the 12-gauge AyA to Europe in early December for some driven shooting, and never noticed much difference between them. Then in January I went to Mexico to hunt quail and took my Fox, partly because I hadn't shot it much lately and partly because it's easier to get good 20-gauge cartridges there than 28s.

I missed the first bird I pulled the trigger on—an easy crossing shot—and the next killed a couple, and went on to miss two or three more, hit one, missed two, on and on. By the end of the day, I was thoroughly disgusted with myself and seriously wondering whether I and this gun had suddenly grown somehow apart. It'd never let me down before, but now it seemed as if our whole relationship had gone sour, that it had for some reason decided to abrogate its place in my quiver. A clear case of arrow failure.

That evening at the lodge, Vicky gave me a few minutes to rant on being deserted by a gun I love, then handed me a drink and a pipe, waited till I was sipping and puffing more or less contentedly, and became, as always, the voice of reason.

I am little competitive in any conventional sense but, as she knows better than anyone, enormously competitive with myself, demanding a level of performance far beyond what I'd ever insist upon from anyone else. In work, in shooting, in golf, pool, in whatever I know I can do reasonably well, I expect a great deal of myself and incline toward self-flagellation when I don't perform as well as I think I should.

Vicky knows this and knows what to do about it. Your gun, she said after a while, hasn't changed. It's as it always has been. So are the birds, and the dogs. Now what's left?

Arrow failure? Nope, Indian failure. If I'd been one of my own students, I would've sorted it all out in a moment: I missed a couple of shots I know I should've hit, and when that happens we all tend to bear down too hard and try to be too precise—which means looking at the gun, measuring, doing way too much thinking and steering and guiding instead of relying on the simple, natural muscle memory that can point a finger with uncanny accuracy right where our eyes are looking.

All true, but for every cause there is an effect, and later, rehearsing with a disinterested eye all the wretchedly blown shots of the day, standing over my own shoulder in the limbo that stands on the edge of sleep, I found the answer.

It was the gun and I, together, neither the one nor the other to the exclusion of all else.

My Fox is the most purely dynamic of all my guns. It generates inertia almost of its own accord, partly from weight, partly from balance. It's like a driver. A driver rewards restraint—swing it at eighty percent of your capacity and you'll love what it does; go for 110 percent and you'll mishit it every time.

And that's my Fox. All the others are happy to be handled, but the Fox likes to show its own life. It's longer than the rest, and more innately dynamic. All I have to do is start it moving and stay with it, and it goes where I look. It's pleased with persuasion, unhappy with force.

Which of course is what I'd been doing—trying to force a perfectly simple act I've rehearsed hundreds of thousands of times. Understanding that, I met the next day with the serenity that makes bird hunting the thing that touches my soul so deeply.

It was a lovely day, warm and dry, and I found myself in the zone: Focus my eyes on the target, swing the gun and point just there, forget about what I know and allow my body to do what it can. I didn't hit every bird I shot at, but I didn't miss any that I shouldn't have, and that to me is a satisfactory level of shooting.

At the end, split off from my partners, I had a hundred yards of thigh-deep grass to cross with the truck in sight. Somewhere near the middle of it, I blundered into the last covey.

They were spread out, feeding, I assume. A half-dozen blew out almost underfoot, which allowed me to get my gun in my hands in time for the rest. I killed two on the next flush, just letting the gun go where it wanted, guided by my eyes, and then a lone sleeper who waited for me to reload. When he went down, I unloaded and went to help the bird boys look, figuring I had been given a gift whose implications I should not ignore.

I'm not so naive as to think I'll never again have a bad day of shooting, but on the other hand, I won't soon forget the lesson. That they are my perfect arrows doesn't mean I can take them for granted and get away with it, or treat them as if they are identical. More to the point, having perfect arrows doesn't mean I can take for granted the expectation that I will handle them perfectly, without regard for the individuality of their own natures.

As I said earlier, having more than one gun is a large part of the pleasure in hunting and shooting, but it does not come without a price. It means that we must take even greater care in our ongoing quest to be perfect Indians.

21

FIT FOR A FITTING

Once upon a time, American shooters looked upon gun fit as some arcane mumbo-jumbo of interest to no one but the British. Nowadays, fit has become almost a cottage industry, with legions of writers on the one hand explaining why it's so important, and a host of would-be fitters lined up on the other, eager to do their thing.

I've already aired my thinking on what a proper fitting is and what it isn't, in the Jan/Feb 2000 issue of *Shooting Sportman*. What hasn't been addressed, at least so far as I know, is the role the shooter plays.

Being fitted for a gun is not like being fitted for a suit, not a matter of standing passively while a tailor drapes and measures your bod. I've heard fitting compared to sighting in a rifle, which is basically true in principal, but grossly misleading when it comes to the actual process.

Fact is, gunfitting is a process and one in which both fitter and fittee play active roles and bear certain responsibilities. If you're determined to be the best shot you can be, you need to be fitted—but by the same token, if you

---

want the best fitting, you need to do your part. Just showing up at the appointed place and time isn't enough, particularly if you show up completely unprepared and with your head full of expectations that may or may not be realistic. The better you do your job, the better the fitter can do his.

So what is your job? And how can you prepare to perform it to your best ability?

Your most important contribution is to have a sound shooting technique that you can perform consistently. I know I said the analogy with being fitted for a suit doesn't apply, but imagine for a moment what the result would be if you assumed a different posture every time the tailor took a measurement. He can make a suit that will look right in different postures only if you give him a consistent model to work from.

Consistency is even more important to a gunfitter, particularly so when it comes to mounting the gun.

My favorite description of a fitted gun is one that points where your eyes are looking when all you do is raise it to your cheek without moving your head. Making it point where you look is the fitter's job; raising it to your cheek, to the same place time after time after time without moving your head, is your job. The fitter can't do it for you, and if you can't do it for yourself, you can't realistically expect a good fit.

Think of your cheekbone ledge as your anchor-point. The fitter can fine-tune your foot position and posture, but if you can't consistently bring the gun to your anchor-point—if your gun-mount is all over the place—he has no basis from which to create a fitted gun.

So, the first step in preparing for a fit might start months in advance. You may need to take some good instruction, and you certainly will need to practice your technique till it becomes second nature.

Talk to your fitter ahead of time. Tell him what your skill level is, and be honest about it. Tell him whether you want to be fitted for a side-by-side or an over/under; for several reasons, your proper dimensions will be slightly different from one to the other.

Ask him how much time you should allot for a good fitting. If he tells you it won't take more than fifteen minutes or half an hour, find somebody else. A thorough job of fitting can take as much as three hours. If you want to be fitted for both an over/under and side-by-side, allow even more time. You can do yourself, and your fitter, a favor by going through a little tune-up drill in preparation. Facing a mirror, hold your gun in a good ready position—the very end of the butt tucked under your armpit, barrels about level, shoulders relaxed, and upper arms at about forty-five degrees out from your sides. Focus on your eye in the mirror, the eye that corresponds to the shoulder you shoot from, and practice mounting the gun by pushing forward with your leading hand, as if trying to stab the muzzle straight into the reflection of your eye. (It's wise to stand far enough back so you don't stab the muzzle into the mirror.)

Some important points here. First of all, don't adjust yourself to the gun; just work on making that smooth, pushing motion with your leading hand while bringing the stock to your cheekbone ledge. Most shooters who've never been fitted have spent a lifetime adapting themselves to their guns. The point of having a fitting is to adapt the gun to the shooter, so don't short-circuit the process by looking at the gun and adjusting to it.

This forward push is the move your fitter should ask you to make when you shoot at a mark on his pattern plate. He won't want you to swing the gun to the mark, because that will create a false picture of where the gun shoots in relation to where you look. It's the reaching, spearing movement, initiated by the leading hand as you bring the stock to your anchor-point, that tells the real tale.

As another good exercise to accomplish the same thing, lay a cup or glass on its side at about eye-level and practice pushing the muzzle straight into the open end as you mount the gun.

Do these exercises for about ten minutes twice a day for a few days before your fitting and the whole process will go a lot more smoothly.

Another important point: Once you've made a gun-mount to the mirror, look at the reflection of the muzzles. If those of a side-by-side aren't perfectly horizontal or if those of an over/under aren't dead-on vertical, you're canting the gun, and that'll make a difference in where it shoots. If canting derives from a poorly fitting stock, your fitter will make adjustments to get rid of the problem. If canting is a flaw in your technique, he'll work with you to weed it out. (The most persistent canters often respond to nothing less than a length of two-by-four applied smartly to the back of the head, but it does work.)

Unlike Arlo Guthrie's advice about preparing for an army physical, it is not a good idea to get snot-flying drunk the night before your fitting. Get a good night's sleep instead and have a light breakfast. If your fitting is scheduled for early afternoon, don't eat a huge lunch; having too much food on board will make you sluggish and less able to handle your gun with skill and precision.

Wear what you wear for most of your shooting—target vest, hunting vest, whatever. Don't be surprised if you fitter digs out some safety pins, duct tape, or whatever it takes to make your vest fit so that you don't snag the gun butt every time you try to make a good mount. You'd be surprised at how many poorly designed, blousy vests there are on the market.

If you want the same gun to serve both in the uplands and for wildfowling, be aware that the amount of clothing you pile on during cold weather will make a gun fitted for autumn shooting seem too long in the stock. Best way to deal with this is to have two buttpads fitted, one that gives you the right length with shirt and vest and a thinner one for when you're bundled up later on.

Wear comfortable shoes, preferably with some lift in the heels. Proper gunning posture has your weight slightly forward, onto the balls of your feel, something like a boxer's stance, and heeled shoes will help you achieve that.

If it's a bright day, wear a cap to shade your eyes—or better yet, a broadbrimmed hat that'll also shield your ears and the back of your neck from the sun.

Thin, close-fitting leather shooting gloves are a big help. You're going to fire quite a few shots in the course of a fitting, and the gloves are good protection against hot barrels and against chafing from the checkering on your stock.

Ear protection and good shooting glasses are absolute, and a responsible fitter will not allow you to fire a shot without them. If you like mufftype hearing protectors, be aware that the muffs you wear for pistol or rifle shooting may not work well with a shotgun. Nothing is more distracting than knocking the stock against a muff while you're trying to make a good mount. If you don't have custom-molded earplugs, use foam plugs; they're as effective as anything at blocking harmful noise.

A proper fitting will have you standing exactly sixteen yards from the pattern plate, and even lead pellets can bounce straight back at you, so shooting glasses are a must. And don't even think about firing a load of steel shot at a steel plate; the pellets can come back at you going damn near as fast as they went forward.

Fitting can be a tiring job, both for you and the fitter. Don't hesitate to ask for a break to sit down for a few minutes, or have something cold to drink on a warm day. And be considerate enough to offer the fitter a break now and then, too, even if you're pumped up and raring to go.

It's okay to bring along one or two of your own guns for impact-testing after the fitter has determined your proper dimensions on his try-gun. Just don't drag out a whole armload of guns and ask the fitter to supervise while you test every one of them. Chances are, your fitter will be gracious enough to accommodate such nonsense, even though he shouldn't. It's a waste of his time, and yours. He's already determined what dimensions you need, and there's nothing useful to be gained in learning that one gun may be only a few fractions off while another needs radical alteration. Dealing with that sort of thing is a stockmaker's job, not a fitter's.

It ought to go without saying, but all too often doesn't, that you should be prepared to do what the fitter asks you to do. You're not there to prove what a whiz-bang shot you are, nor that you know his job better than he does. Try to handle the gun the way he asks you to, be patient, and enjoy the benefit of his experience. You both have the same objective in mind—which is to take you one more step toward being the best shot you can be.

22

A GOOD
CLOSURE

Please don't take this amiss, but I'm going to tell you how to close your gun. It's not that I think you're a dunce who might also need to be told how to tie your shoelaces, but you may not be aware that you can do some real damage to your gun just by the way you close it. I didn't know until someone told me, and it was a lesson I was happy to learn—both for the kindness I can do my guns and for the safety factor as well.

If you want to see some graphic demonstrations of how not to close a break-action gun, visit any trap or skeet club. I don't know why so many target shooters like to close their guns as if they were breeching an artillery piece, but a lot of them seem to. Maybe they think it's part of being an aggressive competitive shot. I do know that the litany of *bash*-"pull"-*bang* makes me happy they aren't shooting my guns.

What doesn't make me happy is when somebody slams one of mine hard enough to make the springs rattle, says, "Boy, listen to that! Locks up

---

like a bank vault!"—and then does it again, enchanted by the Siren song of metal pounding against metal. I'd rather choke than be rude—and I don't mind anyone looking at my guns—but I've got into the habit of saying, "Close it softly, please" when I hand one to someone I don't know.

And then there was the clodpate who worked in a gunshop where I used to hang out about thirty years ago. He thought it was cool to hold guns one-handed by the grip and close them like cracking a whip. He did it once when the owner happened to be around, and snapped the wrist of a 20-gauge Model 21. The ensuing staff meeting was probably audible several blocks away.

So what happens when you slam an action? First, the barrels smash against the breech face, and then the fasteners snap into place under the full force of their springs.

Hammering the barrels against the breech does two things, neither of them good. For one, it can literally peen the surfaces, gradually opening a gap where there should be none. And it needn't be a big gap to cause a problem; a gun is off-face if the breech will close on a .010-inch feeler gauge.

Slamming an action also puts enormous stress on the joint—on both the barrel hook and the pin that together form the hinge. Popular wisdom says old guns that rattle like a bad set of false teeth have "shot loose." It is possible to shoot a gun loose over time, especially on a steady diet of heavy loads, but I'd bet anything you care to name that most loose guns got that way on a steady diet of heavy slamming. If the effect could somehow be measured, it'd be interesting to know the actual equivalency in wear between slamming and shooting; I wouldn't be surprised if it worked out that one hard slam was worth fifty or even a hundred shots.

It's hard on the stock, too—perhaps not always as dramatically as the gunshop incident I mentioned earlier, but as my father used to say, not doing obvious harm to something doesn't mean you're doing it any good.

In some guns, especially over/unders, the stock is attached with a drawbolt that runs lengthways through the wrist. This is a good way of keeping stock and gun frame tightly together, and it also reinforces the stock at its thinnest, weakest point. Slamming probably does these stocks the least harm. But most side-by-sides and some over/unders don't have drawbolts, and slamming stresses them both in the wrist and in the stock head. A crack in either place is serious damage.

Exactly what effect there is in allowing fasteners to snap into place under their spring tension depends on the fastening system.

A lot of side-by-side guns are made with the classic Purdey-style double underbolt, and if all the parts are properly fitted, the top-lever spring, which is the one that seats the bolt, doesn't have to be overly strong to be effective. You can close these guns gently, and the bolt will click softly into place. In fact, most makers who build such guns recommend that you allow the fastener to snap home because it ensures that the bolt is properly seated in its bites.

Guns with rotary top fasteners—A.H. Fox, L.C. Smith, and the Ithaca NID, for instance—are another story. Rotary fasteners want to pop open on their own as the gun is fired, unless all the bearing surfaces are perfectly radiused and fitted (which is seldom the case with factory-built guns) or unless they're held in place by a very stout spring. Next time you're someplace where you can handle one of these guns and a high-quality English, Italian, or Spanish gun at the same time, compare the stiffness of the top-lever springs. The one with the rotary bolt will be noticeably stronger, because it not only has to snap the bolt into place, but also has to help keep it there.

Slamming is doubly bad for these guns. Besides the stress on the breech and the joint, allowing the fastener to snap shut is brutal to the bearing surfaces. They are, of course, tapered to compensate for wear, and there's a good reason for that, because these systems, effective as they are, have a built-in source of erosion.

Most over/unders are fastened either at mid-breech or at the bottom, and you can usually let them click shut without doing any harm. The lever spring is the key; the heavier and stronger it feels, the more care you need to take in closing the action.

The classic indicator of a fastening-system's health is the position of the top lever in relation to the top tang. If it rests right of center, there's no appreciable wear; dead center means some wear; and left of center says you better know a good gunsmith because this sucker's gonna need some attention if things don't change, and maybe even if they do.

What needs to change is how you close the gun. Slamming it shut is, I would hope, out of the question, but you can't even ease it closed and be home free. The best thing to do is close it quietly and use your thumb to brake the top lever as you do. Get into the habit of doing this and you can spare your guns any further grief.

There's a safety issue here as well. I haven't slammed a gun in almost forty years, but I've had two go off accidentally when I closed them and have seen another go off in someone else's hands on a trap field. In my case, the culprits were mechanical—a stuck firing pin and a broken cocking rod. On the trap field, I suspect it was a combination of mechanics and pilot error—a faulty sear that jarred off when the shooter banged the gun shut. Nobody was hurt in any event, but an accidental discharge is scary.

Most shooters close their guns by swinging the barrels up. That's okay if the muzzles are pointed safely, but if it happens to go off, there'll be a shot charge on the loose, at just about the elevation where a dog might be.

The safest way is to leave the barrels pointing at the ground and raise the stock. If it's a gun you can allow to click shut, all you have to do is grasp the butt end or put with your hand under the belly of the stock and lift. It's more awkward if you need to keep your thumb on the top lever, but you can get it done by making a little quarter turn to the side. It takes some practice, but it's a good habit to get into.

Actually, the time for building good habits is now, at home with an empty gun. If part of your preparation for the bird season includes regular indoor swing-and-mount sessions (and I do hope it does), you can simply make closing the gun part of the routine. You'll enjoy the season more if you aren't trying to learn new gun-handling methods in the field. Your gun will enjoy it more, too.

23

A SHOW OF HANDS

If by some quirk of happenstance I was offered the opportunity to live another human lifetime but was required to choose an occupation completely different from any I've enjoyed this time around, I would ask first to be a veterinarian, and if that bus happened to be full, I'd want to be an orthopaedic surgeon who specialized in hands.

Human hands are fascinating, arguably the most complex voluntarily controlled biological structures that have ever existed. Not, perhaps, as complex as the human brain, but the brain lacks muscles—in most cases, anyway—and is subject to a whole range of involuntary functions that hands are not. Hands are it. Hands have made everything from the Pyramids to fine guns—including machines that can in turn make Pyramids and fine guns. Eyes may be windows to the soul, but hands are the soul's agents.

Hands are every shooter's primary connection with the gun. I know I've argued that the crucial contact is between the cheek and the stock, and it's true, but such contact could hardly exist if not for the hands.

Watch any first-class shot (or musician, golfer, baseball player, billiard shot, boxer, or whatever) and you'll see hands under very precise control. The rest of us tend to be sloppy with our hands, even though they're supremely trainable and infinitely willing to do whatever bidding our eyes and minds decree. The best part is that our hands are capable of acting without conscious direction, if only we're willing to spend the time it takes to create in them the memory.

For a shooter, the task is twofold. First, there's the matter of just holding the gun, and then the business of moving it according to purpose. Neither is entirely simple.

I like to watch the students in our shooting schools uncase their guns and put them together. How they handle them tells me something I can use to good advantage later, when the shooting sessions begin. When trigger-time comes I pay as much attention to hands as to feet and posture and all the other basic elements of good shooting.

Guns are made for hands as well as by them, so the nature of the object fits our physical capacities to a great extent, with places specifically designed for a trigger hand and a leading hand. But even that allows for latitude, and latitude always offers an opportunity for something to go wrong.

Some students may think we're just being picky, but Bryan Bilinski and I both call attention to their hands. We want the trigger hand firmly onto the wrist of the stock, as far back from the trigger itself as it can be with the pad of the index finger just touching the trigger blade, with a comfortable gap between the second finger and the trigger guard bow, and with the base of the thumb nestled into the thumbhole of the stock. And we want the trigger-hand thumb wrapped over the top of the grip.

All this for several reasons. The leading hand is important because it controls where the barrels point, but the trigger hand bears the dual responsibility of making sure the stock comb is nestled firmly under the cheekbone and of being able to slap the trigger with the best possible sense of timing and touch. We want the fingertip in contact with the trigger because the fingertip is where nerve endings are most concentrated, as opposed to the crease of the first joint, where a lot of beginning shooters think the trigger should be.

We want the middle finger distant from the trigger guard because if it isn't, recoil is likely to drive the two forcefully, and painfully, together. We want the thumb wrapped over the stock because that sort of grip promotes the most sensitive level of control and also prevents injury. Leaving your thumb on top of the wrist may not feel awkward in itself, but "awkward" does not begin to describe the sensation of having recoil ram the edge of the top lever into the end of your thumb. It is excruciatingly painful and usually bloody besides.

Your trigger-hand grasp should be firm but not so tight that the veins pop out on your forearm. A death-grip restricts both the flexibility of your arm and the precision with which you can bring the stock comb to that magic spot under your cheekbone. Too much trigger-hand grip also promotes too much trigger-hand movement, and the last thing you want is for that hand to control the sequence of swing and mount. Important as its contribution is, the trigger hand has to be the follower, never the leader.

Because the hand that holds the barrels is the key to everything in successful shooting, it, too, needs to find both an optimal placement and grip. To understand where it ought to be, just point your finger at something, anything, and then look at what you've done. Our natural tendancy is to point a finger with an arm fully extended—which is our unconscious way of making the very best use of our natural eye-hand coordination. This is supremely accurate. In fact, if your index finger could fire shot charges or bullets, you'd never miss a target.

So you need to take advantage of that natural accuracy and put your forward hand on the gun in such a way that your arm goes *nearly* straight when you bring the gun to your cheek and shoulder. Nearly straight. You don't want your elbow locked, because that, too, restricts your motion—but you also don't want your hand so far back that it's virtually under your chin, because then your ability to point accurately goes to pot.

How far you put the leading hand out depends upon how long your arm is, of course, and to some extent on the configuration of the gun. The splinter forend of a side-by-side is not meant to be held; you hold it by the barrels, not by the wood. Repeaters and over/unders typically are made so that you do grasp the forend wood. This is good for keeping your hand off the hot barrels, but it also means that schnabel forend tips are often more decorative than practical. For me, that sharp, flared ridge is right where I want to put my index finger, and I haven't yet found a schnabel that feels comfortable. If your gun has one and it bothers you, having the forend rounded off could be money well spent.

Although you want to develop the habit of having your arm comfortably extended, you won't always want to keep it that way. If for some reason you have to shoot with a gun that's either a bit too long or a bit too short, you can compensate to some degree by moving your leading hand. Reaching out onto the barrels farther than usual makes a short stock feel longer; by the same token, you can make a long one feel shorter by shortening your forehand grip.

And there are times when changing your grip is an advantage even with your own guns—which, let's assume, fit you perfectly. Next time you're on a clays course shooting going-away overhead targets that come from behind, extend your leading hand a little more than usual. Swinging a gun downward is an awkward move for most of us, and having some extra extension makes it feel smoother and more controlled. On the other hand, if you're shooting high incomers, either clays or driven birds, do just the opposite and shorten your reach slightly; this, combined with shifting your weight to your back foot as you swing, will keep you from feeling uncomfortably stretched and off balance even when the targets are almost straight overhead.

How your leading hand ought to grip the gun is as important as where. As with the trigger hand, your grasp should be firm. A strangle-hold limits the flexibility of your arm and shoulder, but if I had to choose one evil over another, I'd rather see you holding the gun a bit too tightly than too loosely.

You'll notice a lot of novice shooters simply lay the barrels in their palm, keeping their hand open and fingers off the barrels or forend. Way bad. Having no grasp at all vastly reduces your control over the muzzles and at the same time entirely eliminates the leading hand from playing any role in damping recoil.

The need for optimal control in where the barrels point is obvious. The recoil issue may not be, but the fact is, the leading hand absorbs more kick than the trigger hand does. If you want to demonstrate this for yourself, fire a shot with your arm extended and with a good grip on the barrels, then cork one off without any grip at all. Just please don't do it with heavy loads; you'll notice plenty of difference even with light ones, and I'd just as soon you didn't get your chimes rung at my behest. Better yet, take my word for it, because I've been there and done that and it ain't fun.

In fact, if your favorite gun starts biting your trigger hand all of a sudden, whacking the trigger guard against your middle finger, it means your leading-hand grasp has grown lax, and you can cure it by tightening up.

How you apply the pressure is largely up to you, so long as you don't do it in any way that allows your fingers to interfere with your view down the rib or that cramps your wrist. When I shoot a side-by-side, I lay my thumb down the side of the left barrel, extend my forefinger a bit to enhance my sense of pointing, and apply the actual pressure between my second and third fingers and the base of my thumb—much the same way I grip a golf club with my right hand. My little finger may touch the forend, but it's not on the barrels and doesn't exert any force. That's what's most comfortable for me; you might want to experiment a bit to find what feels best for you.

Because hands are so important, I like to give them every possible advantage and protection. That means wearing shooting gloves. Thin, close-fitting leather gloves greatly enhance your grasp on the gun while at the same time protecting your skin from the abrasion of the checkering and the heat from the barrels. Some shooters like to use a leather-covered hand guard on a side-by-side. I don't; they tend to slip under recoil, and I find that annoying. Some shooters don't like anything covering their trigger fingers. It doesn't bother me, but if it bothers you, you can get gloves that allow you to bare your finger—or you can just do a snip job with scissors.

One caution: Most gloves with trigger-finger slits also have a bit of Velcro on them so you can pin the loose finger back to the top of your hand. I had a pair of those once. As I said, having a glove on my trigger-finger doesn't bother me, so I never pinned it back. But I was wearing them while hunting quail one very cold day and, without thinking, wiped my drippy nose with the back of my right hand. I'm here to tell you that a half-inch square of Velcro hooks feels like a wood rasp against a cold nose. I thought I'd removed a chunk of my schnoz, and I don't think it could've hurt any worse if I really had. I kept the gloves, but the Velcro was history as soon as I found my pocketknife and cleared the tears from my eyes.

Mishaps aside, it's impossible to overestimate the importance of what your hands contribute to your shooting, even though their significance is easy to overlook. Using them consistently well takes some thought and some practice, but the results are worth it. You'll know you're on the right track if you can imagine your gun quoting a line attributed to Mae West: "Oooh. I don't recognize the face, but the hands are familiar."

$$\textbf{(24)}$$

METHODOLOGY

W e have become fond of referring to any style of shooting as a "method." I suppose this goes to an instinctive wish to quantify things. That's okay. As a species, we like to think things thoroughly through, even if it means thinking them to death. In shooting schools, my partners and I point out that we can bring almost anyone within six inches of becoming a world-class shot. Stickler is, those six inches are the straight-line distance from one ear to the other. Some years ago, we invented the perfect shooter: About nineteen years old, in superb physical condition, with an IQ of twelve.

The ability for rational thought is both a gift and a curse. On the one hand, it's the source of virtually all significant human accomplishment, for good or ill. On the other, it's an impediment to some things we'd really like to do. Like shoot well.

So we fasten upon "methods" as a fix. If we could only mimic what the great shooters do—copy their "methods," in other words—then we can all be great shooters, too. And if that doesn't work, then we need to shoot the same brand of gun as the great ones, with the same recoil pad, the same front sight, the same cartridges...on and on.

I don't want to start a semantics debate here, but I would argue that there are three fundamental approaches to hitting flying objects with a charge of shot. Call them methods if you like. To me, they're techniques.

Move a gun along a target's flight path, pass it, stay a given distance ahead at the same speed, track its progress a bit, and pull the trigger. This is called sustained lead. It's deadly as hell at skeet, where you can memorize angles.

Or, move a gun along a target's path, pass it, accelerate beyond, and pull the trigger. This is what's known as pull-away, and it's the ticket for crossing birds at about thirty yards or more.

Or, move a gun along a target's path, swinging it faster than the bird is flying, get ahead of it, and pull the trigger. We know this as swing-through; it's the upland hunter's ideal. Not bad for decoying ducks, either.

Now, what's the common denominator? If you chose option A—move a gun along a target's flight path—you may step to the head of the class. Every so-called method depends upon tracing a line. (I'm not going to get into spot shooting, which belongs almost solely to those who shoot doubles trap. It's an ambush approach and doesn't work very well in the field.) The method that does work begins with tracing a line. What you do once you catch a target is technique, and which one you choose depends upon angle, speed, and distance.

The most famous "methods" are those espoused by great shooters of the past. The two best known are Churchill's and Stanbury's. They are, in fact, virtually identical, defined by the physical characteristics of the shooters themselves.

Robert Churchill was a short, portly man who didn't have much flexibility. In order to shoot well, he needed to move his feet and shift his weight from one side to the other, hence the famous Churchill dance steps. This is not to say that anybody can't benefit from stepping toward a target with his leading foot—especially an upland hunter who's usually caught off-balance when a bird goes up. Churchill, on the other hand, mainly practiced and wrote about driven shooting. With other guns on the line, safety and the courtesy of not poaching your neighbor's game dictate a rather narrow window. Even so, Churchill's build was such that he had to step around in order to get squared up with the birds. It worked for him and works for anyone who is of a similar physique.

Percy Stanbury, by contrast, was a fairly tall, slender, almost cranelike man who could plant his feet and swing a full arc in either direction. He could step if a shot required it, but he usually didn't need to. His accomplishments at both game and clay targets pretty well speak for themselves.

So where do these so-called methods differ? Many take them to be almost mutually exclusive, but the fact is, they simply are accommodations in aid of doing the same thing—move the gun along a flight line, make contact (touch the target, as Jack Mitchell likes to say), swing ahead, and pull the trigger. Dead bird, end of story.

Or maybe not. There is something of value in Churchill's approach. Shift your weight, move your feet, lift a heel, do whatever a target calls for. Any move that helps you keep the muzzles on the flight path with your shoulders level is going to work. If you're built like Stanbury and don't have to move your feet to commit the same move, cool. Just do it. Most people lie between the physical extremes of Churchill and Stanbury, so we spend a lot of effort in schools trying to find what's going to work best for each student. Take a little from here, a little from there, forget about "methods," and the result is a better shooter. That's what we're there for, as we see it.

In advanced schools, we make an issue of the various techniques, showing when the choice among sustained lead, pull-away, and swing-through will make the difference, with emphasis, of course, upon learning to read targets and gaining a feel for what to do according to distance and angle. It takes a lot of practice, but it can be done. All of the really experienced shots I know tell me they choose instinctively and only realize what they've done after the fact.

What they do is choose the point in a flight line at which they actually mount the gun. The swing begins as soon as their eyes can define a path; the mount is when the gunstock comes firmly anchored to the cheekbone ledge. In teaching this, I have borrowed a trick from my friend Gil Ash. He's an excellent instructor and communicates this as well as I've ever heard: Mount just behind the target, right on it, or just in front. Which you choose depends upon which technique is right for a given target.

Some instructors speak of an "instinctive method." In fact, there is no such thing. Instinctive shooting is a reversion to what's most familiar, right or wrong. I refuse to drive in Britain because I know full well that if suddenly confronted with an oncoming car my instinct would have me drive to the right, which wouldn't be a good idea.

To become an instinctive shot requires learning sound technique and then practicing so much that it becomes second nature—until, in other words, you take your brain out of gear and simply allow your body to do what you've trained it to do. If you train it well, it'll do something effective; if not, it will revert to old, bad habits.

And if you're looking for a useful method, forget about Whozis or Whatzis and adopt the one my colleague Chris Batha expresses so nicely: See bird, shoot bird.

Reaching that point takes a lot of work, but in the end it's more satisfying than any amount of mental gyration spent fretting over who says to do what.

25

MAKING ALLOWANCES

$\mathbf{A}$s I describe it to my students, the process of instinctive shooting involves moving the gun from where the target was to where it is to where it will be when the shot swarm arrives. The first two parts of that are simple enough, just a matter of tracing a target's flight path, using the gun barrel as if it was an extension of your finger. Our natural hand-eye coordination allows us to do this very accurately.

It's the last part—taking the gun to where the target will be—where confusion sets in. How do we know where the target will be? How far ahead of where it is when the gun catches up, and how do you measure that distance? Thus the concept of lead—forward allowance, as the British call it—rears its ugly head.

There are four main places where you can miss a target—above, below, ahead, and behind—along with various permutations. You can, for example, miss above and ahead, below and behind, and so on. This is one reason why I insist that bird hunters should learn to trace flight lines;

if you can accurately move the gun from where the bird was to where it is, you've automatically eliminated half the potential misses. If you're on the line and simply extend it ahead of the target, you can't miss above or below, only in front or behind.

Contrary to popular wisdom, more game birds than you'd ever imagine are missed in front, but I'll get to that presently. For the moment, let's think about the misses behind, the ones caused by too little forward allowance.

It's possible to determine lead mathematically. If you know the speed of the shot swarm and the speed, distance, and angle of the target, you can compute the necessary forward allowance right down to a gnat's whisker. This is the basis of the skeet-shooting technique known as sustained lead. It's done by moving the gun at the same speed as the target while holding the muzzle far enough ahead to accommodate the angle.

Most serious skeet shooters use this approach. It works because skeet targets always follow the same path at the same speed, so mastering sustained lead means memorizing the necessary forward allowance at every station, and that isn't particularly hard to do. Shoot ten or a dozen rounds every week, develop a memory for the various sight pictures, and you can become a competent sustained-lead skeeter in a couple of months.

But sustained lead has virtually no application to any other type of shooting. It works for some of the weirder presentations in sporting clays, and you can occasionally use it for pass-shooting doves and ducks—but for the general run of upland bird shooting, it's as useless as cartridges with no shot in them.

Sustained lead is mechanical, and the more machinelike the shooter, the better it works. Game shooting involves far more variables than sustained lead can handle, and it demands more of the shooter. Game birds' speed, angle, and distance are rarely the same from shot to shot. You can't memorize something that continually changes.

Consequently, the one word scarcely ever uttered in our shooting schools is "lead." As instructors, we make sure everyone understands that the gun has to be a certain distance in front of the target, but we never offer any prescriptions as to how much.

Why? Simple. When the shooter himself becomes a critical factor in the process, lead ceases to be prescriptive and becomes instead a phenomenon that depends upon what each shooter sees. And what he sees depends, in turn, upon how fast, or slowly, he moves the gun. The shooter, in other words, is as much a variable as the birds he's hunting.

Every shooter has his most comfortable speed. Some handle their guns quickly (a lot of them too quickly), others are slower, more deliberate. Even taking into account the fact that a shotgunner is working with a shot pattern that may be two or three feet in diameter and is therefore forgiving, the mathematics of forward allowance are the same in swing-through game shooting as in sustained-lead skeet shooting. The difference—which makes all the difference—is what the shooter sees.

Let's give two different shooters the same shot at a pheasant, and let's say the rooster is crossing at right angles about twenty-five yards out and flying at the same speed in both cases. The fast shot might pull the trigger the instant his barrel passes the bird's beak and fold him neatly. The more deliberate gunner might have to see two or three bird-lengths of daylight between barrel and bird in order to achieve the same result. One appears to shoot almost at the bird, the other way ahead.

The difference is gun speed. For the faster shot, the sheer momentum of his gun will take the muzzle to where it should be, so he doesn't need to see much daylight in front. He can appear to shoot almost directly at a crossing bird and hit it. This is the shooter who'll sometimes grin and say, "Man, I killed that one just before I shot it."

He who swings more slowly needs to see a greater separation, needs to move his eyes farther ahead in order that his leading hand will point the gun to the right place.

Bottom line here is that lead of itself is almost meaningless in the practical world of game shooting. Or as Jack Mitchell, the current dean of British instructors, puts it: Lead is speed, and speed is lead.

Learning what relationship between gun and target you, personally, need to see comes only through practice and experience—and you should therefore take well-meaning, and usually unasked-for, advice with a dollop of salt. A naturally fast shot trying to advise a naturally slow one, or vice-versa, is a recipe for frustration all around.

I said earlier that more birds than you'd guess are missed in front. These are the birds that fly away at a shallow quartering angle—which is the most common shot in the uplands. These birds play with your head. They appear to be escaping in a huge hurry, so they tempt you into shooting in a huge hurry, using too much speed or too much gun movement or both.

Here's where everybody, especially the naturally fast shot, needs to chill out and slow down. No bird alive can fly faster than a charge of shot, so it's not getting away nearly as quickly as you think it is. It's also moving at such a shallow angle that the necessary "lead" is practically non-existent. If it's angling left, focus on the left wing (or on the right wing, if it's going right), move the gun in a relatively slow, short swing, and pull the trigger as soon as you catch up to the bird. It'll look as if you're shooting right at it, but the small amount of momentum from a slowly moving gun will build in exactly the forward allowance you need. Don't just poke at it, and for heaven's sake, don't aim. Spot-shooting is never consistently successful, and aiming is a sure ticket to missing behind.

On the other hand, if you move the gun too fast at a quartering bird, the chances are excellent that you'll blow right on past and miss it in front. Regardless of the angle, and regardless of your natural gun-handling speed, keep your eyes focused on the target. Looking at the gun, even just a quick glance, is a habit that bedevils an enormous number of shooters. They're trying to be too precise, trying to be sure the gun is exactly where it should be. Problem is, if you look at the gun while swinging it, you'll slow it down or stop it altogether.

Keep your eyes locked onto the target. You'll still see the gun in your peripheral vision, and that's good enough.

Forget about "lead." Practice until you have a clear sense of what you need to see in order to accommodate your particular gun speed. Swing the gun and pull the trigger when everything looks right. Don't second-guess yourself. As I tell my students, when it looks right, it is right, and it won't get any righter. Stop dithering and fiddling around, and just shoot the damn thing. That is the point, after all.

26

SWING, MOUNT, AND SHOOT

Economy of motion is essential to any athletic act. Whether you're trying to hit a golf ball, a tennis ball, a cueball, a clay target, or a game bird, you'll be most efficient when you do only what you need to do and nothing more.

The typical shooter makes too many separate moves. He bangs the gun-butt to his shoulder with his trigger hand, drops his head to the stock, and then goes chasing after his target. Not only is this too much motion, but most of it works against a successful shot.

Letting the trigger hand take charge moves the wrong end of the gun at the wrong time, making the important end—the muzzle—bounce all over the place. Moving your head momentarily short-circuits the accuracy of your eye-hand coordination. Having to chase a target means you're less likely to catch it, or else likely to go too far past it because of excessive gun speed.

There is no economy of motion in a mount-and-swing sequence, but you can achieve economy if you turn it around and make it a single motion of swing-and-mount.

You point the gun with the hand that controls the muzzle. That's your leading hand, and it should always be in the lead, with the trigger hand following behind. The shot goes where the muzzle goes, so the first move you make should be with the leading hand, taking the muzzle toward the target, right along its flight line. If you allow the trigger hand to take over at any point, the muzzle will go off the line.

The trigger hand does have an important job, which is to raise the stock right to the ledge under your cheekbone while you keep your head dead-still. If you touch the stock to your cheek consistently, you can forget about the butt—because it will automatically go to the same place on your shoulder every time. But it won't if you go to your shoulder first, and the muzzle won't stay on the target's path if the leading hand isn't leading from start to finish.

Timing is part of economy, and the best rule of thumb for shooting is to make haste slowly. Nothing does more mischief to making a good shot than rushing it. Smoothly and accurately tracing a flight line with the barrel is far deadlier than any hurry-up poke—and you almost always have more time than you think.

If you move your leading hand first and let your trigger hand follow, the muzzle should be just behind the bird when the stock touches your cheek. Then all you have to do is keep your forward hand moving through the bird and past its beak, and pull the trigger.

The better able you are to turn an inefficient mount-swing-shoot sequence into a compact, one-piece move of swing-mount-bang, the better your economy of motion will be. And the better that is, the more likely you are to put the shot where the bird is.

Watch an untrained shooter trying to hit game birds or clays, and you're almost certain to see him slam the gun to his shoulder, drop his head to the stock, and then go chasing after a target that he's very likely going to miss.

Part of the problem is that he's making three separate moves where he should be making only one, but his most serious error, the one that does the most mischief to his attempt at making an effective shot, is moving his head.

Shooting a shotgun is a pure exercise in hand-eye coordination. You don't aim a shotgun—at least not if you intend hitting a moving object. You just point it, exactly as if you were pointing your finger, tracing the target's path from where it was a moment ago to where it is now to where it will be a moment after you pull the trigger.

It's as simple as that, and it works because the human brain provides us with an extraordinary ability to point a finger precisely where our eyes are looking. If you could fire bullets or charges of shot out of your index fingers, you'd never miss anything. Normal hand-eye coordination is enormously accurate—but unfortunately, we often short-circuit our natural gift.

Hand-eye coordination works both ways. You can point a finger in a direction you're not looking, turn your head, and focus precisely on whatever is straight beyond your finger. Or you can focus your eyes on something and point right at it without having to look at your finger—without, in other words, having to aim.

But something has to remain stable; we can look where we point or point where we look, but either the hand or the eye has to be still in order to be accurate. As shotgunning is the art of hitting moving objects, the hand obviously has to be moving as well, which puts the burden of accuracy on the eyes—or more properly, the head.

I demonstrate this to my shooting students with a little exercise that you can do, too, right now. Focus your vision on some small object across the room and, keeping your head still, point at it. Notice how wonderfully accurate you are. As I said, if you could fire shot from your finger...

But then put your head in motion—side to side, back and forth, around and around—keep it moving, try pointing at the same object, and you'll see instantly how a moving head wrecks your ability to point with any accuracy at all.

A still head allows our eyes to focus precisely, but it's effective only if the eyes are focused where they ought to be. And that's on the target.

Looking at the gun is the most common visual error shooters make. Even expert shots do it once in a while; poor shots do it a lot. You can accurately track a moving target only when you're looking at it. Our eyes can't focus in two planes at once, and for a shotgunner, the target's plane is the only one that matters.

To see what happens when your focus shifts, find someplace where you can see traffic moving along a highway in the distance. Pick a car, focus your eyes on it, and follow it with your finger. As long as you stay focused on the moving object, you can trace its path smoothly and keep pace with it easily. Now do it again, but this time deliberately shift your focus back and forth from a car to your finger and see what happens.

Every time you look at your finger, your hand either slows down or stops altogether. Your gun does exactly the same thing when you look at it. You can't drive a nail while looking at the hammer, nor hit a tennis ball when you're focused on the racket. Nor can you consistently hit flying targets when your head is moving or you're looking at the gun.

(27)

Touchy-Feely Stuff

Trust me, I'm not sitting here surrounded by candles glowing through a haze of incense smoke, wearing a headband and tie-dyed caftan, or listening to Ravi Shankar on the CD player. Nor am I going to break into a chant in the middle of this. I am, however, going to talk about shooting as a matter of feel.

Shooting is an athletic act, and to become truly competent at any athletic act, you have to commit its component parts to kinetic memory. It has to become ingrained in your muscle memory to the point where you no longer have to think about what you're doing, but simply feel it. This is the key to success in everything from swinging a golf club or a tennis racket to casting a fly line or driving a nail. If it feels right, chances are it is right. If it doesn't, the results probably aren't going to be what you want.

Of the fundamental elements in shooting, the swing and mount is the one you need to feel most keenly. Swinging the gun and bringing the stock crisply to your cheek is the most dynamic aspect of shooting flying and therefore the most important. You can have your feet all wrong and be off-balance, but if you can make a good swing and mount in spite of it, you still have a better-than-even chance of making an effective shot.

The multi-phase mount-and-swing a lot of shooters make must surely feel as awkward as it looks. And it looks like an unfolding lawn chair: Whip the gun-butt to your shoulder (which can make the muzzle dip so far that it's almost pointing at the ground), bang your head down onto the stock, make a twitchy little motion to get lined up with the rib, and then start looking frantically for a bird that by now is either out of sight in the woods or just crossing the county line.

The first step is learning a sound technique so that your leading hand always leads, your trigger hand maintains a subordinate role from start to finish, the first motion you make with the gun is the beginning of the swing, and your head stays dead still.

All this is easier to demonstrate than to describe, so you may need to take a lesson or two from a good instructor in order to know what you should be doing. Then you have to practice it enough that muscle memory can take over and you can operate by feel rather than thought. It's a bright spot for me in any lesson when somebody executes the technique, smokes a target, and then says, "That felt just right."

Of course it did. And once you know how it should feel, you'll know instantly when you're doing it wrong. And what you feel, right or wrong, will be some component of the swing and mount, of how your body relates to the gun. It's also a bright spot in a lesson when someone bungles a shot and says, "Nah, bad gun mount." That tells me the feel is starting to develop.

In his excellent book *The Inner Game of Golf*, Timothy Gallwey says, "My experience is that if there is an important flaw in the swing, the part of the body that is critically related to that error will draw itself to the student's attention. On the other hand, if there isn't an error, generally the part of the body that is critical in controlling the optimal swing, will receive the student's focus and be reinforced."

The irony of shooting is that the leading hand is not our dominant hand, so that the first part of Gallwey's postulation isn't quite as apparent as he suggests. Using too much right hand seldom catches a right-handed-shooter's attention. It feels completely natural, even though it's wrong. But if I can make him sufficiently aware that his left hand is the one that needs to be in charge, then Gallwey's second notion is true as rain. If he says, "That felt exactly right," and I ask what part of his body felt particularly right, and he says, "My leading hand," then I know we've made a breakthrough. If he'll practice to the point where that feeling becomes second nature, he will become a deadly shot.

And he will remain so as long as the feel remains current. Feeling, however, can be fickle, can betray us on a moment's notice, particularly when subjected to the overwhelming weight of too much thought. Miss a shot or two you know you should've hit, and you'll start thinking about it. Miss another and you'll bear down even harder with all the weight of your analytical mind. At that point, the skill you've worked so hard to learn is flirting with the kiss of death.

Jane Frost, a Massachusetts golf instructor, uses a concept I find very useful in shooting. She calls it Home Base, and it amounts to an awareness of how the golf swing feels when you do it right. Same with a gun. Think of how it feels when you make a perfect swing and mount—then quit thinking and concentrate on the feel. Groove that into muscle memory, and you'll always have a Home Base you can return to.

Every shooter experiences the occasional slump. It may be a matter of four or five bad shots in a row, or it can take on epic proportions and last for days, even weeks. One English instructor I know describes this by saying, "His technique has deserted him." To my mind, it's the other way around. The shooter in a slump has deserted his technique, and the shortest route back to Home Base is to remind himself how it feels when he does it right. Not how it looks or how it sounds or smells, or what he thinks, just how it feels.

If you and your gun suddenly lose that lovin' feeling, there are several ways of getting it back. When I miss a shot or two that I shouldn't have missed, I like to spend a few minutes practicing the swing and mount with my eyes closed. If I'm not distracted by pointing at anything in particular, the feel of how I should be handling the gun usually is easy to recapture. (I sometimes shoot as if I had my eyes closed, but that's another story.)

My friend Chris Batha, chief instructor for E.J. Churchill, Gunmakers, taught me a wonderful little trick. Hold your gun as you normally would, and pull backward slightly with your trigger hand while pushing forward slightly with your leading hand, as if you were trying to stretch the gun.

Then practice your swing and mount a few times, moving slowly, maintaining the tension between your hands. You needn't use a lot of force; even a little tension is excellent for reminding your muscles of how your hands should be properly working together, and how it feels to your arms and upper body.

If you have more than one gun that fits you well, switching guns sometimes works wonders. Except for properly matched pairs, every gun has a slightly different feel to it. Familiarity with the feel of a certain gun does not necessarily breed contempt, but it can breed sloppy handling. Having something unfamiliar in your hands can help you back onto the right track, just by heightening your awareness of what you should be most aware of.

Having been a young man in the 1960s, I confess a certain nostalgia for the doctrine of touchy-feely stuff that was popular then. And I have learned that feel is more useful than I ever would have guessed, even in those tactile days. That the mantra now has to do with a 20-gauge instead of a daisy chain is all right with me. It's nice to know there's something I can do better now than I could when I was young. Hell, some days, just being able to feel anything is enough to be grateful for.

$$\left(\begin{array}{c}28\end{array}\right)$$

THE EYES
HAVE IT

Certain questions continue to puzzle me. Why, for instance, did World War II kamikaze pilots wear helmets? Do dyslexic women shout "Oh, dog! Oh, dog!" at certain times? If it's called tourist "season," why can't we shoot them? And why do shotguns have sights?

In the latter case, the only answer that makes any sense is simply that it's traditional. Next time you're in a museum that has a good collection of antique arms, check out the blunderbusses. These were guns mean to scatter projectiles over the widest possible area at very short range—and on nine out of ten you'll find a tiny bead on the bell-shaped muzzle.

In those days, the British gun trade typically called a front sight a "view nail." "Nail" was the common term for any screw, pin, or peg. The "view" part is self-explanatory. The problem lies in viewing the nail.

From a mechanical perspective, a game gun is an irreducible quantity. There are no extraneous parts. Remove anything and something won't work as it should. Except for the damn sight. You can dress it up—make it of brass, gold, silver, ivory, or even a precious stone—but you can't make it useful.

What you can do is make it an enormous handicap to good shooting, because anything that tempts you to move your visual focus from the target to the gun is a certain ticket to a miss. I can think of one good purpose for any of the various neonlike front sights that are touted as the be-all and end-all of shotgunning: They would be a godsend to turkey hunters in the low light of early morning or dusk.

That's because turkey hunting is not wingshooting, or usually not. Turkey hunting is aiming, wingshooting is pointing, at best as simple as pointing a finger. We will not sneer at turkey hunters because they are aimers, no more than we would sneer at anyone who has the skill to place a bullet in exactly the right place on a white-tail, an elk, a pronghorn, or a prairie dog.

But when the target is a fast-moving object, regardless of whether it's made of clay or covered in feathers, the shooter's eyes are his path to success—and all too often his road to failure.

Success comes from using your eyes like lasers, locking onto the leading edge of a target and then, if the target's angle and distance demand it, having the faith to shift your focus from there to where that target will be when your shot swarm arrives.

The longer I teach shooting, and the more I talk with other instructors, the more convinced I become that shooters make three fundamental errors with their eyes.

One is simply a lack of focus. When a student makes a marginal hit, taking the front, the back, the top or bottom off a target he might as easily have centered, I often ask, "Did you see where you hit it?" If he tells me where, then I can make some physical corrections to get him where he wants to be (though I never interfere when someone makes a solid head-shot). If he says no, or says he didn't see the tiny chip flying off some part of the clay, then I have to find some way of improving his concentration and focus.

Another error is perhaps not so much a matter of vision as of separation anxiety. Long targets, especially long crossers, require a lot of visual distance if the gun is going to be where it needs to be. We all see our guns, ideally in our peripheral vision. One of the tricks we teach is to encourage shooters to put the fuzzy barrel ahead of the sharp, hard target. Sometimes, on a really long crossing shot, both barrel and target have to go fuzzy, and that can be a fiendishly hard thing for some shooters to do. Some shots require our eyes to focus on the sheer nothingness where the gun needs to be in order that the shot and the target arrive at the same place at the same time. To do so is to make an act of faith, to simply swing the gun into space and trust that it's going to turn out right.

My favorite trick to help someone overcome the anxiety of momentarily losing the sharp visual focus I've emphasized so firmly is simply asking him to deliberately miss it in front. Doesn't matter where the shot goes, so long as it's ahead of the target.

A couple of years ago, I worked with a chap who was having a hell of a time with a high crosser. There was nothing wrong with his technique; he just couldn't bring himself to separate the gun far enough from the target. It was one of those slightly overcast days when it's relatively easy to see a shot charge in the air, and I could see his passing consistently about three feet behind. Finally, I told him to concentrate solely on missing in front, and I'm not sure I've ever seen a look of such utter astonishment when he turned the next target into a dustball.

The shot goes where your eyes go, because your hand will point where your eyes are looking. That's the single, simple secret to shooting a gun.
The ones who drive us nuts in school are the aimers. These are guys, and occasionally gals, who simply cannot bring themselves to believe that you can hit a target without sighting. They've been trained, or trained themselves, as rifle or handgun shooters, accustomed to lining up sights in order to be ultra-precise.

It's sometimes a job to convince them that they don't have to be all that precise with a shot swarm that's three feet wide, but when it happens, it's as if the skies have opened and the angels have begun to sing. The most common and most gratifying response to getting someone to take his eyes off the gun, onto the target, and start smoking them is, "I can't believe I'm doing this!" Sometimes, shooting a gun is like falling in love; the less you try, the better it gets.

All these matters are visual—not seeing sharply enough, fearing to lose clear sight of a moving object, and looking at the gun instead of the target. In a way, training to shoot is a matter of overcoming visual habits that are nothing short of sloppy. I reckon we use about fifteen percent of our visual capability in everyday life. Unless it's threatening—like a car suddenly veering into our lane of the road or a toddler poised at the top of a flight of stairs—we tend to see everything instead of anything in particular. You can merely glance at some object, look away, and still reach out and pick it up without fumbling.

The natural coordination between our hands and our eyes allows this, just as the natural coordination between our hands and our eyes allows us to successfully swing a gun on a moving object—except in the latter case you can't simply glance and hope for much success. There, success requires focus, and focus requires some effort.

Back in the days when my job was to teach college freshmen the fundamentals of writing, one of my favorite exercises was a peculiar form of torture that I called The Photographer and the Painter. Pick a scene, preferably a simple one, and describe it in minute detail, capturing everything, just as a photographer would be obliged to do. Then see it with a painter's eye and describe only those details that truly communicate the nature of the scene.

I suspect I was burned in effigy more than once over that one, but I've never found a better way to demonstrate the difference between looking and truly seeing. Shooting is no different. You can look, take a basically aimless poke, and once in a while something will break or fall out of the sky. But mostly not. If you want to hit what you're shooting at, you have to see it, and see it more clearly than anything else around.

I hope you will, of course, look first to see where your partner is and where the dogs are, but once you've decided it's a safe shot, that bird should be the only thing in your visual world. If you can concentrate your focus that hard, you're going to put something into your game bag.

You can tip the odds in your favor with a couple of visual tricks. Clay-shooting coaches talk about finding a visual point in your setup; it's the place where your eyes are able to turn a target from an orange streak into a real object with hard edges. It's a different place for everyone. The most futile thing you can do in target shooting is look at the trap, figuring to see the clay as it comes off the arm. A few truly gifted people have eyes that can focus that quickly and sharply. Ted Williams, and my father, could see the stitches on a baseball coming in at 80 miles per hour or better. My young friend Chris Smith can read a ball because he can see the pitcher's fingers at the moment of release.

The rest of us are not so gifted, so we need to let a target come into our realm of focus, wherever that happens to be. If it's a clay, that will be some distance away from the trap. If it's a bird flushing from the ground, that should be somewhere between waist-level and eye-level. Sometimes you get to spot a bird before it flushes—a skulking pheasant, a woodcock that decides to walk ahead of a pointing dog, a chukar that's behaving like a chukar—but if you think back and compare the number of times that's happened with the number of times you have subsequently missed, you'll get an idea that it's better to let the bird come to you, visually speaking, than going to the bird.

The impulse to look for a bird on the ground, or a target coming off a trap, is easy enough to understand, rooted in a fear that not seeing it at the earliest possible moment means it's going to get away before you can make your move.

Sometimes it does, as in ruffed grouse, woodcock, and a covey of quail in the woods. Then you shrug, smile, and remember that it's called "hunting." More often, you have a lot more time than you think. Ever blown two frantic shots at a bird and then realized it was still well in range?

Making the best use of the time you have begins with your eyes. You can't consistently hit what you can't see, so your first move needs to be a visual lock-on. Think of yourself as a basilisk, the mythical animal that can kill with a look. Find a phrase to run through your mind that brings your reaction under control. The British have a nice one for a flushing bird: "Oh, what a handsome fellow you are." A brief moment of tribute to a lovely bird, a moment to gather yourself for the best effort you can make, a moment in which the eyes have it.

(29)

LEARNING
TO READ

Learning to read is an essential skill. It's as important for a shooter as for a schoolchild. The shooter has to learn how to read a flight line.

For a bird hunter, flight lines are not so difficult. Most game birds flush up and away. The exceptions that come to mind are a second shot at a mourning dove, a woodcock twisting up through treetops, and snipe—a bird my old friend Charley Waterman once described as appearing to fly with one wing at a time. Can't do any better than that.

Otherwise, game birds are straightforward. You might be tangled in an alder swamp, lugged up in doghair popple, in brush up to your neck, or astride a cactus, but that's your problem to solve. The bird simply behaves according to its lights, and its lights tend to shine in straight lines.

At this point, you're reading distance and angle. Speed doesn't have much to do with it. Upland game birds fly at pretty much the same mileage, especially when you boot them up and watch them go. They can't outrace your shot charge.

Get the distance and angle, and you have a bird in the bag. Reading that is mostly experience. Be there often enough, and you'll get it right, like as not.

Shooters go down on clay targets, especially those who haven't shot a lot of them. It's not a character flaw, just a lack of experience. What the inexperienced shooter sees in a target is speed. Speed breeds panic, and panic is not conducive to good shooting. If the majority of my students ever get together and write my epitaph, I imagine it'll be "Calm down and slow down." I know I sound like a broken record, but they get so wound up by the illusion of speed that they become paralyzed and can't hit the ground with both feet, much less a target with a gun.

Skeet and trap are straightforward enough, but now that most clays courses have bought into goofy targets, reading is all the more important. A high incomer that's curling a bit one way or the other can change from a three o'clock leading edge to five o'clock in just a few feet, or from nine to seven if it's going the other way. And to have any expectation of hitting it, you're going to have to see the difference as it happens and adjust your swing accordingly.

A lot of targets, even the dopey ones, have a flat spot in their flight lines. If you see it, the shot becomes a piece of cake. At the first Vintage Cup, at Addieville East Farm in Rhode Island, Geoff Gaebe set up a devilish pair—a long, slightly falling right-to-left crosser that didn't appear to be dropping because of the ridgeline in the background, followed by a dropping incomer on the left. The crosser baffled nearly everyone, myself included, but the incomer had one momentary spot where it was simply hanging in the air. You could stand there all day, shoot right at it at the proper instant, and never miss.

Oftentimes, a complex target offers more than one opportunity, and you make good advantage of that if it's a course that allows full use of the gun (FUG, for short), which simply means you can take two shots at any single target. Fail to read these accurately, and you'll end up fugged for certain.

Once teaching a school in Utah, we had a nifty crosser that came off a ridgetop from the right, looped down and landed about twenty yards in front of the shooter. One of our guys was having trouble with it and was getting frustrated, so I threw three or four for him so he could just look at it without the pressure of being behind the gun.

He finally saw what I was hoping he'd see without my having to tell him. The thing came off level for about the first ten yards—a perfect swing-though shot. If he missed that one, he could dismount the gun, switch to a form of sustained lead, and take it on its way down. He tried it both ways and smoked it every time. From then on, he became a reader.

Sometimes you have to stretch a bit beyond what you think you can do, trusting that your gun and cartridges are up to the task. They always are. No game bird or target can outfly a charge of shot. They might get away by dodging behind a tree, but a thirty-mile-per-hour bird isn't going to outrun a shot charge that leaves the muzzle at 800 miles per hour or better. Trust in that and you can extend your reach.

This is not to advocate skybusting or taking shots that are simply foolish attempts laden with nothing but vain hope—but if you develop a skill at reading flight lines at the same time you enhance your skill in handling a gun, you'll be surprised at what you can do. There's an old adage among British shots that you should never let the bird drive you back. This refers to shooting driven game, and simply means taking your shots at incoming birds before they're directly overhead and thus about to put you off balance.

Reading an incomer isn't always as easy as it might seem, because they're usually curling a bit. You need to keep your eyes locked on the beak (based on the premise that where the beak goes the butt is likely to follow), swing the gun freely, and not be afraid to shoot when he's well out in front. If you follow the rules of taking no shot below 45 degrees or if the bird isn't surrounded by sky, you won't endanger the beaters and will be pleasantly surprised at how far out you really can kill an incomer. I've watched some truly expert British guns who dropped nearly all their birds in front of them. Most of mine fall behind me, but that's just the way I shoot. Sometimes it's easier to preach than practice.

Professor Harold Hill, however, commented that three-rail billiards requires a cool head and a keen eye, and I have written about a gazillion words that those same qualities are sovereign in shooting. The point here is that just focusing on a target isn't necessarily enough. It's essential to focus, but until you have something to focus on, like a flight line, all the focus in the world won't do you much good. And that's where learning to read becomes important.

(30)

SIN AND
TEMPTATION

We all love looking at guns. If we didn't,
we wouldn't spend ungodly sums having them engraved, inlaid with precious
metal, stocked in walnut as dazzling as a prairie sunset, or refinished when
time and use has dimmed their aesthetic glow. If all that beauty is resided
solely in what beauty does, we really wouldn't care whether we owned a Fox
or a Parker, a Fabbri instead of a Superposed, or this in place of that. We
would not admire the artistry of a Harry Kell, Ken Hunt, Winston Churchill,
Firmo Fracassi, Giancarlo Pedersoli, or dozens of others. The best action fil-
ers and stockmakers would be little more than blacksmiths or mechanics if
we did not discriminate among the nuances of grace and form.

All guns are utilitarian; fine guns are a visual feast as well. They are be-
witching, flirtatious as sheep. Fine guns tempt you to look at them, and it's
mostly a temptation for which capitulation represents no sin.

What could be more innocent than gazing at a lovely gun in front of
a cheerful fire, accompanied perhaps by a dog snoozing on the hearth rug,

some tasty tobacco smoldering in a good pipe, and a glass of peaty whisky at your elbow? It's the stuff of dreams.

I love looking at my guns after I've given them a thorough cleaning, like to hold them at arm's length and admire how the workshop lamp limns their elegant lines, makes their engraving sparkle and their walnut glow.

I look at my gun when I slide it out of its case first thing in the morning, feeling the hope that birds are waiting somewhere nearby.

I often look at my gun when I'm sitting on a log or leaning against a fencepost, easing my knees and enjoying a pipe in a spill of sunlight.

These are harmless indulgences, temptations that can be accommodated without need of repentance.

Which is good, because I can resist anything but temptation, and it's nice to have found one that doesn't carry some dire consequence.

Except when it does. There is one time when looking at your gun is both the ultimate temptation and the ultimate sin, bound to bring every-thing to ruin—and that's when there's something in the air that you intend to break or kill. Look at your gun then, and you're courting a wreck.

The human eye cannot focus in two planes at once. You can look at the target or you can look at the gun. You can't do both at the same time, and if you choose the latter, the consequences are as immutable as gravity: Look at a moving gun and you will cease moving it, either momentarily or altogether.

You can consistently hit a moving target only with a moving gun. Occasionally you can get lucky and successfully spot-shoot targets at certain angles, but if consistency is the goal, then movement is the key, and looking at the gun is the arch-enemy of motion.

In Scotland last fall, I spent a morning at the Jackie Stewart Shooting School at Gleneagles, working on high incomers in preparation for a few days of pheasants in East Lothian. After dumping a perfectly good charge of shot ten or twelve feet behind a target that looked the size of an aspirin, I cursed myself for having looked at the gun and remarked to the instructor that he probably saw a fair number of shots like that one in the course of a day.

"Aye," Alistair said, "it would make our jobs easier if we installed a big neon sign out in front of every station, so all we had to do was push a button and it'd light up, saying, 'You missed it behind.' That's where most of 'em go."

Right on. And to "You missed it behind" I would add "because you looked at the gun." That's usually why it happens.

Missing behind derives from a form of separation anxiety, a psychological barrier. We want to see both the gun and the target in the same view. You can't do that with a very high target or a long crosser; you have to track it, catch it, and then look so far ahead that the target fades into peripheral vision. At that moment, the temptation to look at something concrete becomes almost overwhelming, and because the gunbarrels are right there under your nose, it's damnably hard to keep yourself from glancing at them, or worse, focusing on them altogether.

If you were far enough ahead to begin with, a quick glance means a miss just behind. Focus sharply on the barrels, and it's a miss way behind.

On some close-in shots, and all quartering angles, we can see both gun and target at the same time, but you have to focus on the target and keep the gun in your peripheral vision. If you focus on the gun you'll still shoot behind, but instead of a clean miss, there's a good chance of putting a few pellets into a bird—too far back to have much immediate effect but effectively killing it, unrecovered, in the long term.

I wish I could tell you a surefire way to avoid looking at your gun. Having nothing more on the rib than a tiny metal bead, or no bead at all, is some help. Certainly, you don't want one of those ridiculous Day-Glo doodads that shines like neon. It's hard enough to keep from looking at the barrels as it is; the last thing you need out there is some silly contraption that calls attention to itself. Fact is, there is no sovereign remedy short of absolute concentration on the target every time you pull the trigger.

Fact also is, everybody looks at his gun now and then. Beginners do it a lot. But it's a temptation to which even seasoned shots sometimes succumb. In one wretchedly notable instance this season, I looked at my gun five times during one three-day hunt. Five damn times. Three of those birds I killed with the second barrel, one I missed twice, and the other flew off while I stood there with my jaw hanging because I just couldn't believe I'd missed such an easy shot.

One of the most useful things a gunner can learn, something we emphasize in our shooting schools, is to recognize why he misses. Nobody hits every bird or target, but if you know what you did wrong you're much less likely to make the same mistake twice in a row. So, I can tell you why I've missed any given shot and tend to be philosophical about being off balance or making a sloppy gun-mount or swinging too lazily. These things happen, and I can live with them.

But nothing aggravates me more than knowing I've missed because I looked at the gun. That makes me turn red in the face and speak to myself in very coarse language. It's a rookie blunder, and there's no excuse for it. My guns fit perfectly; all I have to do is make a good mount, point my leading hand where my eyes are focused, and that's where the shot goes. Besides, I know how to shoot. After all these years and hundreds of thousands of cartridges, a bird or target in the air ain't my first rodeo. I know what to do and, more to the point, what not to do. I know better than to look at the gun—and yet I still do it, more often than I'd ever wish. The fact that no one is immune doesn't make it any less maddening.

Understanding why we look at our guns is simple enough: We're trying to measure forward allowance, to be sure we have the gun a certain distance ahead of the target. But why do we do it when we know full well that "lead" is entirely a function of gun speed and that trying to measure is the kiss of death to a successful shot? You got me. Call it a brain-fart.

I do know—and this is the worst of it—that an experienced shot is most likely to look at his gun under two circumstances. One is when he's shooting poorly, and the other is when he's shooting well.

I'm not making a joke. Miss, for whatever reason, a shot or two that you know you shouldn't miss, and you'll start looking at the gun just to be damn sure you're far enough ahead—which, of course, is absolute assurance that you'll start missing farther and farther behind. And the more you miss, the more you bear down to prevent it—the classic example of a vicious cycle.

Ironically, you can also be mightily tempted to look at the gun when you're shooting well. Hit five or six birds in a row, to the point where you're feeling well-nigh invincible, and next thing you know, just hitting them isn't enough. You want to center each one. Instead of staying loose and letting a three-foot shot swarm do its work, you start thinking, aiming, handling the gun as if you were shooting gnats with a .22, because you don't want to break this lovely streak of good shooting. When that mindset takes over, you are going to look at the gun sooner or later.

As I said before, I wish I knew of a simple way to forever eradicate this sort of thing from your shooting, but short of submitting to a lobotomy, I don't know the answer.

I do know what's going to happen, though. The bird season is still open as I'm writing this, and I'm going to Idaho next week for three days with pheasants and gray partridge, and at some point I will commit the mortal sin of shotgunning. Having done so, I will suggest to myself that I sit down somewhere, look at the goddam gun till I've memorized every detail, and can start shooting as if I'd actually had a gun in my hands once or twice before.

That'll work for a couple of hours, or maybe the rest of the day. But sooner or later, I'll look at the gun instead of the bird, miss a shot that a blind man shouldn't, and howl like a ruptured coyote.

By all rights, some sins should become less tempting with advancing age; in my case, one or two actually have, but not that one. It's not fair. Besides, any sin ought to at least feel good while you're committing it.

(31)

ON THE
FLIP-FLOP

Shooting, as we all understand, is an exercise of eye-hand coordination. We lock onto a target with our eyes, then move our hands (and the gun, of course) along its flight line to the place where the target will be when the shot swarm gets there. It's a wonderfully simple, completely natural gift that is invariably accurate when wrapped in a sound technique and not disrupted by too much mental gyration. You can't think a target to death, although you certainly can easily think yourself into a miss. Better to simply see the bird and shoot it.

Seeing can be problematic. Let your visual focus lapse even for a moment, and you'll make a shot that pleases no one except the cartridge makers. Trouble is, even consistently hard focus isn't much help when the two sides of your body are struggling with one another for control.

Except in very rare instances, we each have a dominant hand and a dominant eye. Even those who are truly ambidextrous—better than ninety-five percent of whom are women—still tend to favor one hand or the other.

If that hand happens to be on the same side of the body as the dominant eye, no problem. If not, big problem. That's called cross-dominance, being right-handed and left-eyed, or vice versa. This is not uncommon, especially among women. (This isn't the time to offer a neurological explanation of why women are so often ambidextrous and cross-dominant. Suffice it to say there is one, and it amounts to more evidence that women are neurologically the superior gender.)

Men can be cross-dominant, too, and that can make for some major-league frustrations. Shooting from one side while the opposite eye guides the gun makes judging a proper relationship between gun and target hellishly difficult. You can go through your whole life cross-dominant and never know it—until it comes to shooting a gun. You can become highly proficient with handgun or rifle using your opposite eye. Riflemen are wont to close one eye anyway. We don't do much that requires strict coordination between hand and eye on the same side of the body, except wingshooting. And there the requirement is absolute.

The first instructional thing we do in our Fieldsport Wingshooting schools is to check for eye anomalies. For this we use Bilinski's Patent Eye-Dominance Evaluator, a highly sophisticated instrument that has proven extremely accurate over the years. Once we've identified the problems, we bring in the solutions.

One is simply to squint or close the opposite eye. It works, but we don't recommend it. Shooting is a two-eyed exercise. Closing one robs half your peripheral vision and most of your ability to judge distance and angle. Shooting with both eyes open is always better, if you can take cross-dominancy out of play.

Some British gunmakers invented various gadgets and gizmos that were meant to be attached to the gun. These would block the off eye when the gun was mounted. I suppose they worked, more or less, but we don't favor doodads when there are simpler solutions.

A spot of translucent tape in the proper place on one lens of your shooting glasses will do the trick nicely. So will a little smear of anything from facial oil to Chap Stick. I'm a great fan of Chap Stick, myself. I always carry a tube in my pocket anyway, and besides keeping my lips moist, it'll solve an eye-dominancy problem in about five seconds.

A few shooters, having just learned of their cross-dominancy, have asked how long they'll have to wear the tape or the smudge. The answer is forever, unless their dominancy changes or unless they want to go back to shooting as ineptly as they have till now. All we can offer are remedies, not cures.

Dominancy is not a matter of which eye is stronger, but rather of which eye focuses first. The difference in time may be nanoseconds, but for most of us it's there. In my own case, I'm strongly right-eyed, though my right eye needs much more correction than my left, always has. But that one is still dominant.

Instances when both eyes focus at the same time are rare but do exist. This is called central vision, and it can play just as much hell with two-eyed shooting as cross-dominancy can. Time was, the standard remedy was a stock carved so the rib essentially aligned with the shooter's nose. The bend is about half as pronounced as a full cross-over stock—but if you run across one you'll know instantly what it is. An old friend of mine had one built in London years ago, and I shot a couple of rounds of skeet with it just to learn how it felt. *Weird* is the best word to describe it, but I found I could actually hit a few targets. Dunno who was the more surprised.

But times change, and over the past few years we're seeing more and more shooters who exhibit some form of central vision. It's not the true quill, in which both eyes are consistently in charge all the time, but rather a case of both eyes focusing almost at the same time, an initial focus to the bridge of the nose followed by a slight drift to one side or the other. The Bilinski Patent device shows this unmistakably.

But why? What's changed? After talking with a lot of students who demonstrate the tendency, and a lot of time talking between ourselves, Dr. Bilinski and I have concluded that it's a learned response, an actual, though passive, training of the eyes. Nowadays, more and more people spend more and more time staring at computer screens from a distance of about eighteen inches or less, and we reckon this has over time evened out their eye dominancy. One chap told us that he'd spent his whole career looking through the eyepieces of binocular microscopes, and that seems likely to have a similar effect.

These people still have dominant eyes, but those eyes require just a skosh more time to assert themselves.

A recent letter from Mr. Jim Unger of Washington state brought all this into focus, no pun intended. Mr. Unger wrote to ask what he might do about what he nicely describes as "flip-flop" vision—a literal change in eye dominancy from one day to another, or even from one shot to the next. As you might imagine, this can be horribly frustrating. It's also an effect that can result from several causes.

Gun fit is one. A stock that's a bit too low at the face can virtually bury your eye and encourages a habit of mounting the gun anywhere from your jaw to some random spot on your cheek. Make a proper, solid mount to your cheekbone ledge and you may find yourself looking at a top-lever or the back of a receiver. In that event, your opposite eye can take over unconsciously because you really want to see the target.

Besides inconsistent gun mounting, fatigue might be the culprit. Our bodies can get tired in a long round of clays or a long day in the field, and our eyes get tired, too. The concentration of hard visual focus exacts a price.

Age is another factor, one that every shooter has to face eventually. The older we get, the more time the lenses of our eyes require in order to focus. The interference with shooting can be a sometime thing or can amount to a permanent shift in dominancy.

I wonder if weather can affect dominancy, as well. I have only a single personal anecdote to go on, but I do remember hunting pheasants one miserably cold South Dakota day, one of those lovely days when every weed and blade of grass is rimed with hoarfrost. By mid-afternoon the cold was reaching bone-deep. Next thing I knew, I was decidedly left-eyed, and keenly aware of it. It was rather scary. I tried squinting, but I've always shot with both eyes open, and trying to remember to close one only screwed up my instinctive rhythm. Suffice it to say, I didn't hit a bird the rest of the day.

That evening, after a hot shower, a drink, some dinner, and feeling nice and warm, I went out to the gun room and did a few swing-and-mount exercises. Right-eyed again, as if nothing ever happened. It's never happened since, but still I wonder. If extreme heat can affect our vision, why not cold as well?

And there's another possibility, which for want of a better term I'll call acquisitional dominancy. In this, the eye that first sees the target can take over and remain dominant through the shot. For instance, show a right-handed (and right-eyed) shooter a left-to-right crosser and his left eye picks it up first. Control usually shifts unconsciously during the swing and mount, but that might not happen when the eyes are struggling with one another.

My best advice for dealing with the flip-flops is to first have your gun fit and the consistency of your mount evaluated. If that's not the gremlin, then smudge the off lens of your shooting glasses. A little dab of Chap Stick, just enough to keep that eye subordinate, should do the trick.

I suggested this to Mr. Unger, who wrote back to say that it appeared to be working for him. To which I say, good-o. In shooting, as in most things, I'm all in favor of what works, especially if it's the simplest solution. Occam's Razor continues to apply.

Vision is possibly our most complex and delicate sense. We rely upon it in myriad ways all the time. We can train it and refine it to special situations and purposes. But in shooting, seeing is not always believing. So maybe there is after all something more than a joke in the husband's universal question: Who're you gonna believe, me or your lyin' eyes?

AUTHOR'S NOTE: Unlike many of the marvelous things you see advertised on television, the Bilinski's Patent Eye-Dominance Evaluator is sold in stores— supermarkets, mom'n'pop groceries, convenience stores, all kinds of places. It's simply the cardboard tube from a roll of paper towels. Use it correctly with the help of someone who knows how to evaluate the results, and you can identify eye anomalies in short order.

We do ask a ten-cent royalty for use, but so far that remains on the honor system. Our royalty negotiations with the manufacturers aren't getting on well.

(32)

A Step in Time

Taking a short step toward a target gives a shooter a tremendous advantage. I've mentioned this before—but over the past couple of years I've delved quite a lot deeper into understanding how such a simple move can have such a profound effect.

And the effect can be profound, at least to the extent of spelling the difference between a hit and a miss. Which in shooting is about as profound as it gets.

Stepping is nothing new. It's an old English pheasant shooter's technique. Jack Mitchell showed me how to do it many years ago. The problem is that you don't need it at clays or skeet or trap, and most field shooters don't know the move—even though it's one of the deadliest moves a bird hunter can make.

Some years back, in our continuous process of refining the Fieldsport shooting schools, my partner Bryan Bilinski and I decided that we needed to introduce some element of movement. Nearly all our clients are bird hunters; they come to us to shoot better in the field. We can teach our basic technique quite well by getting them lined up perfectly on a target before it flies, but we felt we could do them even better service by adding something a bit more birdlike. Hence the step became part of the program. Somehow, it devolved upon me to teach it, so I spend the second day working with each group of shooters on a skeet field, putting some body dynamics into the process.

The step is simplicity itself, although its implications aren't. I get my shooters somewhere on the field that offers a crossing shot, have them set up their feet at right angles to the target's flight line, heels right together, and show them what to do with their feet when the target appears.

If we could turn a book page into a video, I could show you this in about ten seconds, but we can't so you'll have to bear with me. The foot in question is your leading one, the one that is on the same side of your bod as your leading hand—the left if you shoot right-handed, the right if you shoot from the left. For the sake of keeping verbiage (and possibly garbiage) to a minimum, I'll describe it for a right-hander.

The first move you make is not with the gun but rather with your leading foot. Your leading hand follows closely behind, but the foot initiates everything. And all it has to do is make a short step and point its toes at the place you intend to break a target or kill a bird.

Two key elements here. First, it is a short step, no more than six or eight inches, and your heel might not move even that far. In the beginning, a lot of shooters want to step way out. I had one chap a few years ago who looked like he was trying to do the splits; getting him to shorten up took some work, but we finally managed. The problem with taking too long a step is that you disrupt your balance. Moreover, your whole body goes down, and if you've properly picked up the target's flight line, that sudden drop can make your vision go momentarily wanky, which doesn't contribute much to completing a smooth, unhurried shot.

The other key is pointing your toes. This is extremely important. Just stepping to the side does nothing but widen your stance. That in itself isn't necessarily bad, but it doesn't get you physically focused on the target— which is the whole point of stepping in the first place. A lot of shooters have trouble with toe-pointing at first, but that's only because they've never done it before. Once they get the feel of what we call the Fieldsport Dance Step, lights start coming on.

Remember now, the step is always with your leading foot, regardless of whether a target is flying right to left or left to right. On a left-to-right you simply cross your left foot in front of your right. This might feel awkward at first, but trust me, trying to step with your other foot will put everything out of whack. You may need to lift your right heel as you come around; that's perfectly okay. Just don't try stepping out with your right foot.

Taking the step accomplishes three things, all of them good. As you step toward your chosen kill zone, your body pivots and that starts the gun moving. (This presupposes a good ready position, with the butt under your arm and the barrels just above horizonal.) Getting some momentum even as you begin the gun mount may mean having to slow your swing and mount just a bit, but I have seen few shooters who didn't benefit by taking off a little speed.

Pointing your toes brings your weight down just where it needs to be—on the ball of your leading foot and not on your heels. We compare proper shooting posture with a boxer's stance, with your weight just slightly forward. You can keep better balance, move more smoothly, and recoil won't feel nearly as harsh.

Stepping is a means of facing the target. You don't shoot a gun across your chest, as you would a rifle. If you face the target, your shoulders can stay level. Apart from sloppy gun mounting, I probably see more misses by guys who've developed the habit of dropping a shoulder rather than pivoting their bodies. I ran into one chap who had it so badly that he actually leaned sideways from the waist. Wasn't pretty, but we finally got it fixed, and in one day he went from Mediocre-minus to a solid B-plus.

When a shoulder comes down, the barrels start moving in a rainbow arc, which means losing the flight path of the bird, which in turn means missing underneath.

Do not, incidentally, take the notion that rainbowing your barrels will help you hit chandelles on a clays course. There's a whole separate technique for those doofy things; we can get into that some other time.

So how do you learn the step? A little instruction from someone who really understands it wouldn't hurt—but don't assume that everyone who calls himself an instructor knows the tricks. Even the best clay shooters probably don't know much about it, because there's no real need for it in their sport. But it's a dandy thing for a bird hunter.

You can start incorporating the step into your routine as you do your periodic swing-and-mount exercises indoors. Move your foot first and let your leading hand follow. Just keep it short and point your toes. In the end it should become one compact, economical move from your foot to your cheek. Certainly you can practice on a skeet field; set up with your feet pointed the wrong way and work on stepping into the shot. You'll like it come dove season when the little guys try to screw you into the ground. You'll like it, too, when a grouse or pheasant decides to go somewhere you don't expect. Which of course is one reason why we go looking for them in the first place.

(33)

No Quarter Asked
or Given

The nature of upland game being what it is, and the way we hunt being what that is, the most common shot in the uplands is at a bird going away in a shallow quartering angle. Over time, these shots outnumber the combined total of crossers, hard risers, corkscrews, chandelles, skips, dips, dives, didoes, and other avian aerobatics by a factor that I reckon would go well into double digits.

Not hard to figure out why. A bird's instinct is to get away from you. If it's trying to get away from your partner or your dog, it may present you with anything from a straightaway to a kamikaze aimed at your eyebrows, but it's still operating under an impulse to fly away from whatever it perceives as a threat.

Birds that occupy relatively small home ranges—bobwhites and ruffed grouse, for instance—have a highly developed sense of escape routes, and if you get between them and the sanctuary they have in mind, you can get buzzed. But even in cases when the instinct to flee is shaped by a desire to flee along a certain route, what starts as an incoming target almost always turns into a going-away shot. I have yet to see the man quick enough with a gun to do anything but flinch away from quail hammering around his ears or a grouse that flushes right up his nose. If you shoot at all, you turn around to do it—and there's the same outgoing, quartering angle you would've had if you'd walked in from the opposite side.

The thing about the quartering angle is that it's both the easiest and the hardest shot you'll ever see at a game bird. The easy part has to do with the angle itself and the fact that no bird can fly faster than a charge of shot. Forward allowance typically amounts to mere inches.

The hard part is a matter of inches, too—the five or six that represent the distance between a shooter's ears. The quartering shot is difficult because we make it so.

How often have you popped off a quick shot at a departing bird, wide open, watched it keep going, and wondered how you could possibly have shot behind a straightaway? The answer is right there in the question, hiding in a thicket of assumptions.

Assumption 1: A going-away bird is flying so fast that it's going to escape in an instant.

Assumption 2: Assumption 1 being the case, you'll never have a chance if you don't shoot as fast as you can.

Assumption 3: If you miss, you miss behind.

Assumption 4: Any going-away bird is going straight away.

The problem is, none of these are entirely true, especially in the case of a quartering shot.

Going-away birds look like they're going hell for leather, and they are—but only in their terms. Bobwhites can fly about 55 miles per hour, pheasants about 70, but neither one reaches top speed within the first 30 or so yards after they flush. Quail can accelerate a bit faster, so let's say that from the ground to the outer edge of gun range neither bird exceeds 30 mph. That's 44 feet per second.

Let's also say that your shot charge leaves the muzzle at 1,200 fps. That's 818 mph. Which one is going to outfly the other?

Making a faulty assumption about the speed of the bird leads directly to an equally faulty conclusion about how you should handle the gun. If the bird's going fast, the gun has to go faster, right? Yes, but the lateral distance is what's important. Remember, it's the shot charge, not the gun, that has to catch the bird. A target traveling a shallow quartering angle offers so little lateral movement from the shooter's perspective that the gun needs to move very little, and it certainly doesn't need to move fast.

Unfortunately, that's exactly what a going-away bird tempts you to do—go after it in a headlong rush with a big, fast, loopy swing. This amounts to too much gun speed and way too much barrel movement, and that is the kiss of death to a situation best handled slowly and with as much economy of motion as you can bring to bear.

If you've operated according to Assumptions 1 and 2, you will inevitably fall victim to Nos. 3 and 4 in trying to assess what went wrong.

For one thing, a true, dead-bang straightaway shot is very rare. Birds and clays alike almost always offer a bit of angle—maybe not much, but it's usually there. That means you have to swing the gun. But if you swing the gun fast and far—and don't stop it by looking at the barrel—your chances of missing behind are almost nil.

And maybe "swing" is the wrong word, because it conjures the image of more movement than this sort of shot needs. Visualize the layout from an overhead perspective, and you'll see what I mean. Because of the angle, the target's flight line from the shooter's point of view is extremely short—and a short flight line requires a short gun movement.

So what happens? This is the part that boggles beginners (and quite a few experienced shots who haven't thought it through): Miss a quartering shot and the odds are about ten to one that you've missed it in front. By this I mean missing a bird or target that's angling slightly right to left by shooting too far to the left side, and vice versa. Ever shoot at a quartering-away bird and just break a wing? We all have, usually the wing on the side that represents the bird's direction—and that means you almost missed it in front.

The margin for error on a quartering shot increases geometrically from the gun muzzle to the target, so every inch of lateral muzzle movement becomes many inches at target distance. That's why too much gun speed makes it so easy to blow right on past.

This is also why the fabled speed of a short-barreled, lightweight gun is more bane than boon. The faster the muzzles are moving, the more precise you have to be in pulling the trigger at just the right instant. Be late by only a few milliseconds and you'll shoot way in front.

If a short, light gun magnifies the error of too much speed, a longer, heavier one accentuates the problem of too much movement. The more momentum you generate with a long swing, the more likely it is to pull the gun too far past the target.

In sum, too much gun speed makes you move too far, and moving too far before you catch the target creates too much speed. Together, speed and movement conspire to wreck your ability to pull off what actually is a very easy shot.

The key to consistency with these, regardless of the gun, is to do just the opposite of what your mind may be telling you to do.

It starts with your eyes. When you react in a panic because you think the bird's escaping at warp speed, your visual focus isn't very precise—and a quartering angle requires more precision all around than any other shot. Look for and focus on the leading edge, the left side if it's quartering left, the right if it's going the other way. With a bird, it's useful to focus on one wing or the other, especially if you can't see its head.

Move your leading hand in a slow, short, precise motion to where your eyes are looking, and *shoot right at the target*.

I don't mean stop and aim at it; I mean pull the trigger the instant you see the gun catch up with the target. You'll see the barrel in your peripheral vision while you remain focused on the target, and you'll know when the two come together. The picture you want to see will look as if you're pointing right at the bird—which in fact is exactly what you're doing at that instant. If you keep moving the gun at the same slow speed, the forward allowance will be exactly right by the time your trigger finger responds to your brain and the shot charge gets to where the bird is.

Think "half-speed," "slow motion," or whatever works to keep yourself from making a rush at the target. This is crucial. The gun only needs to be moving fast enough to catch up with the target, and on a shallow angle that isn't very fast at all. Slow, slow, slow.

And keep it short, short, short. Watch a good shot go after quartering clays and you'll see very little barrel movement, eight or ten inches at most. If you're hunting and have to turn in order to take a quartering shot, move your feet first, then the gun; don't mount it and make a big roundhouse swing as you turn. That won't work.

Now, if you need to demonstrate for yourself that I'm not talking through my hat about all this, here's what you can do. In some safe place, hang a clay target from a fence wire or on a post, whatever, just so it's dead still and you can see it clearly. This represents what you see on a going-away shot.

Back off about 20 yards and shoot it while swinging the gun from one side to the other. First, start your swing from 10 or 15 feet to one side, swing fast, and pull the trigger when you think you can hit the target. Don't slow down as you approach it; just keep swinging fast. Try that a few times and see how many you hit.

Then start with the barrel closer to the target, move slower, and see how much easier the whole thing becomes.

If your local clays course doesn't have a variety of quartering presentations, a skeet field is a great place to practice—especially High House Nos. 1 and 2 and Low House Nos. 6 and 7. It's also a good place to practice your footwork if you're tuning up for game shooting. Set up so you're facing at a right angle to the target's line, and step toward it before you start your swing and mount.

If your visual focus is as sharp as it ought to be, you'll be able to see where you hit each target, and that'll tell you what you're doing right or wrong. Shooting the left side off a target at Low 7, for instance, means that if you'd moved the muzzle just one more inch, it would have been a clean miss in front. Excessive speed is the usual bugaboo, so if in doubt, slow down.

When you reach the point where you're making smokeballs with nearly every shot, carry the same speed and rhythm to the game fields. And keep in mind that overtaking a 30-mile-per-hour bird with an 800-mile-per-hour shot charge does sort of put the odds in your favor. All you have to do is make sure they occupy the same space at the same time.

(34)

INCOMING!

Everyone has a favorite shot. It usually is one we hit more often than we miss, because nobody likes to miss, no matter how philosophical we are about such things. But it also is a more or less demanding shot. Powdering umpteen-dozen gimmes in a row gets tedious after a while. Good shooting thrives on a challenge.

My favorite is one that most shooters seem to either love or hate. Not many tread neutral ground over incomers. These are the tower shots on a clays course, Low 1, High 7, and Station 8 at skeet, driven pheasants and partridge, doves, ducks, whatever tends to fly high and fast and is willing to come over the gun.

Those who harbor dark feelings toward incomers are, not surprisingly, those who've had little opportunity to practice the shots and no instruction on how best to handle them. Incomers are different from quartering shots and crossers and demand some special technique.

The setup is the same as for any shot—feet no more than shoulder-width apart, leading foot slightly extended and bearing a majority of body weight. But there the similarities end. In the ready position, you should hold your muzzles high, just below the level at which the birds will first appear. This will eliminate wasted motion when it comes time to track the target and mount the gun. In game shooting where birds come out of a wood (or a copse or spinney, if you're in Britain) your muzzles should be about treetop-high—with the butt tucked lightly under your armpit, of course.

Rushing is one of the common errors we see in school. Shooters get all in a swivet and want to track the target with the gun mounted, and thus mount way too soon. Which makes wandering the barrels off-line to the right or left very easy. You may see the target for what seems a long time, but you need to kill it in one short, economical motion, so that you pull the trigger just a moment or so after the stock touches your cheek.

This doesn't mean standing dead still and flailing away at the last moment. This, too, is a form of rushing, and the gun is apt to go out of control. For schools, we launch the incomer from the top of a tall hill, and it's visible for a relatively long time. Rather than letting shooters snatch the gun to their shoulders the moment the target appears, we insist they track it with the leading hand only, moving the muzzles just a bit faster than target speed, and not mount the gun until the target is in killing range. This gives the shooter something useful to do while at the same time gets the barrels moving as they should.

The actual mount should be no more hurried than the initial tracking motion. As the leading hand is already moving, it's a simple matter to push the gun slightly forward, and let the trigger hand raise the stock to your cheekbone ledge. Properly done, it will feel as though you set the butt gently onto your shoulder. No rush, no wobbling or bobbling, eyes locked onto the leading edge, pass the target, pull the trigger, dead bird.

The technique for accomplishing this involves moving your whole body, not just your head, and shifting your weight from your leading foot to your opposite heel. This is the only shot where we allow any weight shift. Go back onto your heels for a quartering-out or crossing target and you'll lose your balance and shoot too high. For an incomer you should let your weight transfer from the ball of your left foot (assuming you shoot off your right shoulder) to your right heel. If lifting your left heel helps with this, it's okay to do so. Just don't let the bird drive you backward; this will happen if you wait till the target is nearly overhead before taking the shot. Here again, you'll go off balance.

Some shooters want to anchor their feet and track the target by bending backward at the waist. This is a mightily awkward move that restricts your ability to pull through the target. Jack Mitchell refers to it as the Three-P Fault—that of Pointing Private Parts. Use your feet to move your body, and take the shot well out in front.

Good visual contact is as important for an incomer as for any other angle. A crosswind can make a clay target or a game bird bend its flight line, and you have to move the gun with it. And you'll have to concentrate in order to keep focused on the leading edge of a curling clay. Birds are a bit easier, because an incomer's head is fully visible—and as we point out in school, where the head goes, the butt is sure to follow. If you make sure your focus is on the head instead of the tailfeathers or wings, you can make good use of the old English pheasant shooter's formula for tracking an incomer—Butt, Belly, Beak, Bang.

Getting the gun past the beak is a problem for shooters afraid of losing sight of the target. Really high birds and clays—say, forty yards or more—often require that you blot them out with the barrels, simply because of the necessary forward allowance. Hitting these demands an act of faith in your technique and gun fit. You can keep sight of those closer in with peripheral vision or with your subordinate eye. If you don't have an eye-dominance issue and can shoot with both eyes open, it will seem as if you're looking right through the gun barrel. You're actually seeing the target with your subordinate eye as your master eye guides the gun. It's one of the advantages of having binocular vision.

If your local clays course doesn't have a tower, you can practice incomers with a portable trap, especially if you can set it up so targets appear over the top of a hill; this is a highly birdlike presentation and offers the trapper good protection besides. You can also get good practice on a skeet field. Position yourself directly under the high-house target's flight line and stand about midway between the center stake and the low house.

Above all, don't be intimidated by incoming targets or birds. Learn the technique, keep calm, and chances are good that they'll become your favorite shots, too.

35

ONE SHORT, SWIFT, HONEST CHANCE

There are times when shooting is a Kodak Moment—when you have about $\frac{1}{125}$th of a second to get some lead in the air or lose the opportunity altogether. Quail present that sort of shot, especially in the brush, and so do woodcock, in some coverts more often than not. And grouse, oh my. Grouse are possibly the finest of all practitioners of the fleeting moment—ruffs, spruce grouse, and blues can disappear in a blink through a maelstrom of leaves, branches, stems, twigs, boughs, and garlands of vegetation. They call the tune, and if you don't boogie on their time, you end up dancing by yourself.

The time-honored approach to dealing with this sort of thing is known as the snap shot. It's a shot that has to be taken very quickly if it's to happen at all. But merely flinging the gun in the general direction of a departing bird won't get it, because it's also a move that has to be performed properly if it's to be effective. And the snap shot can be highly effective.

Not every time, mind you. Some shots are doomed before they even

191

present themselves. If you're just too far off balance or so tangled in brush and doghair that you can't move the gun precisely to the bird, it ain't gonna happen. You may be responding to the behest of nature and find yourself unable to drop one gun and grab another quickly enough. Or you may simply be taking a little mental vacation right when some bird decides it's time to split. Don't fret over these. They happen, and they're part of why it's called "hunting."

Other times, however, you really do stand a good chance of connecting with a very fast shot, and how often you convert these to birds in the bag depends on several things, some physical and some mental.

On the physical side, you need eyes that can focus quickly and reflexes that can take your hand just as quickly to where your eyes are looking. In this, people vary. Older eyes tend to focus more slowly, and older bodies often don't respond with the same speed they once could. There's nothing to do about that but accept it. On the other hand, focus and reflex don't necessarily slow down at the same rate as the rest of the system. At 55, I find that my eyes are still quick and that my hand can respond about as fast as it ever did—even if nothing else does.

Some people, too, are possessed with extraordinary gifts. I've never seen anyone who could shoot any faster, with deadlier effect, than Dan Carlisle. His visual acuity and reflexes are exceptional, enough superior to mine that I could never quite match his speed—but in a few coaching sessions, Danny proved to me that I can be quicker than I thought I could, and that was the first step toward getting a handle on the snap shot.

To understand the nature of the beast, it's useful to recognize what it isn't. A good snap shot is not a spot shot, not a matter of just poking the gun straight to where you hope the bird's going to be in a few milliseconds. That can work on a true straightaway or a very shallow quartering angle, and it can be made to work on targets that are unvarying and completely predictable, but spot-shooting can never consistently produce success with the myriad angles that game birds present.

Likewise, a good snap shot certainly is not the desperate, spastic, Hail Mary twitch of the trigger finger that's usually performed while the gun is nowhere near the shooter's cheekbone ledge and his mind is as chaotic as a hot-wired snake. The only beneficiaries of that little comedy are the bird itself and the ammunition manufacturer.

A good snap shot is a purposeful, fully designed move performed at the maximum speed that does not exceed the limits of a shooter's control.

Control is the key, and as with any effective shot, it begins with the eyes, ends with the hands, and involves the conscious mind to the least possible extent. That's the mental aspect I mentioned earlier.

Technically, there's no essential difference between a snap shot and one taken at a bird you've watched fly in from a half-mile away. In either case, tracing the target line with the gun is the only reliable means of success. The snap shot merely abbreviates the technique. You still have to swing the gun from tail to beak to the space the bird will occupy when the shot charge gets there. The difference is that you have to do it very quickly and with complete mental abandon. Try to think a snap shot, even for a split second, and you're sunk.

Obviously, you'll do this best with a gun that fits, one that points where you look without your having to look at it, because the key to the snap shot is to nail the target with your eyes and let your hands respond instinctively.

With a shot that offers more time, you can sometimes score a hit even if your visual focus or your gun mount is less than perfect. Not so with a snap shot. Because it has to happen so quickly, it has to happen flawlessly.

So what can you do to better your chances? For one thing, you can train yourself to focus your eyes sharply and very specifically. Don't just look at the bird; look at its head.

Oh, c'mon. Half the time you can't even see a grouse's head; all you can see is a vague outline behind a screen of branches.

True enough. But if you force yourself to look for its head, your visual concentration is likely to be even keener than it would be if you were looking at its head. I'm not saying it's easy; focusing that sharply takes energy and effort, but we're all capable of it, and the better you can do it, the better your snap shots will be. Any time your visual memory is of having seen a grouse's tail, your cognitive memory is almost sure to be of a bird you probably could have killed but didn't.

Best of all, nearly everyone has access to an excellent place to practice snap shooting; you'll find it at the nearest skeet field, on the dreaded Station 8.

Actually, the first spark of an idea for this essay came to me while reading a little op-ed piece in the July 1933 issue of *Hunting and Fishing*. (I'm not really that far behind with things; I'd copied the page for another reason. In correspondence and current literature, I'm only eight or nine years in arrears.)

Anyway, the gist of it was an explanation for why the shot exists in the first place. Station 8, the writer says, "is, and always has been called, an 'enforced snap shot.' To force the shooter to break the target before it has traveled its first, or fastest, twenty yards, was the one logical and simple way to give the Skeeter a snap shot, whether he liked it or not. The snap shot is part of the education of every upland hunter in the game field. Station Eight is a good liberal education along similar lines: that is, the shooter is given no time to correct his aim, but is presented with one short, swift, honest chance to get his gun to his shoulder and shoot. No station on the Skeet field will teach a shooter quicker gun handling, nicer or quicker coordination of visual and manual dexterity."

I agree wholeheartedly with the spirit of this, if not entirely with the language. I cringe whenever anyone mentions the word "aim" as something a shotgunner ought to do, and if I had my way, talking about getting the gun to the "shoulder," as opposed to the cheek, would be the Eighth Cardinal Sin. (Skeet was originally a low-gun game, and still was in the 1930s; it didn't lapse into mounted-gun monotony till later, when bozos obsessed with scores ascended to a majority.) Moreover, I would argue that no station on the skeet field—or any other target field—"teaches" anything. All it does is offer an opportunity to learn; only a teacher teaches.

Fact is, for someone left to his own devices in figuring it out, Station 8 can be the most devilishly frustrating thing anybody ever thought of doing with a shotgun. There you are, 22 yards in front of a trap that's about to fling a target your way at roughly 60 miles per hour, and you have to hit it before it gets past. To beginners, it's impossible, a circus shot, a trick shot, unfair, unrealistic, cruel, unusual, yadda, yadda, yadda—but once you understand what's required, it becomes not only supremely makeable, but also truly one of the best tests of "visual and manual dexterity" you could ask for.

It is the perfect snap shot, pure coordination between the eyes and the hands, admitting nothing else. Apply even the slightest amount of thought and you've missed it. Hesitate for the twentieth part the tithe of the merest fraction and all is lost.

But grab it with your eyes, point at the front edge with your leading hand as the stock snugs to your cheek, and pull the trigger at the same moment, and you can make smokeballs at Station 8 all day long. Apply the same technique, the same haste under absolute control, to game birds, and you'll be a better snap-shooter than you ever thought possible.

Here's the drill. Get a skeet field to yourself, just you and one or two like-minded partners, and start with Low House 8. High 8 is the same shot, but the flight path of Low 8 is easier to visualize because it's more obviously rising. If at all possible, do this in late afternoon, when the sun's at your back (good skeet fields are laid out east and west), so the only color you see on an orange-topped target is the leading edge. It's orange, everything else is black, and that helps.

Start without the gun. Have someone release a few targets while you work on focusing your vision sharply on the leading edge. Get your eyes locked onto that orange edge until it seems to glow like neon. Once it does, the target will magically slow down and appear to come floating out like a butterfly the size of a trashcan lid.

Then add the all-important leading hand. Call for some more targets and point to the leading edges. Don't just poke your finger at them; point by lifting your hand from the bottom edge to the top edge, tracing the flight line in a short but positive move.

Now you're ready for the gun. Set up properly, with your feet side by side, the leading one pointed a few feet left of the trap, your weight forward, chin level with the ground. Take up a good ready position, with just the end of the stock tucked under your armpit, shoulders relaxed, elbows about 45 degrees out from the vertical line of your spine.

Clear your mind completely; live entirely within your eyes and your leading hand.

Say "pull," fasten your eyes on the front edge of the target, lift your leading hand, point it right where your eyes are looking, feel the gun at your cheek, and pull the trigger.

The first few times, you'll probably be distracted by the idea of trying to hit the target; you'll look at the gun, and miss behind. Relax. Forget about ideas. Forget about trying to hit anything. Just concentrate on pointing at the leading edge, and it's yours.

Once you find the groove, you'll notice that the snap shot is a lot like a chip shot in golf, a move performed with the hands and arms while everything else remains still. As in chipping, proper set-up and balance are important, of course, but the actual shot is all in the arms.

Ah, yes—but how is one to get set up and balanced when the very nature of the snap shot dictates maximum speed? There's no time to get set up.

Actually, there is, in most cases, anyway. Sometimes you just have to tip your hat to a bird that's caught you out, but more often than not, you have more time than you think. If you're hunting with a dog, you should be able to anticipate the opportunity for a shot, and that in itself is an advantage. Moreover, game birds do not take off at anywhere near the speed of a clay target, and if you can reach the point of consistently crushing Station 8s, birds are a cinch by comparison.

You can get set up and balanced very quickly by stepping toward the bird with your leading foot—the left one if you shoot right-handed—just before you start moving the gun. With a bit of practice, you can do this even before you see the bird, can train yourself to step toward the sound of its wings.

You can develop this skill on a skeet field, too. Once you've learned how to whack low-house targets while standing on Station 8, start from Station 1 and walk toward Station 8, and let the puller release targets at his discretion. The sound of the trap will be your cue; when you hear it, take a step with your leading foot, find the target with your eyes, and take the shot. The more you refine, through practice, your visual focus and your economy of movement, the easier it all becomes.

The chap who wrote the little piece in *Hunting and Fishing* that I quoted earlier says in conclusion, "Once mastered, Station Eight...is good, sound, and pleasantly spectacular snap-shooting." This is certainly true as far as it goes, but by using Station 8 as the means to a different end, "pleasantly spectacular" doesn't even begin to describe the feeling you get from smoking some wily old cock grouse who's made a career of baffling hunters with a high-speed disappearing act.

Better still, it's one thing to bask in the afterglow of a nicely executed snap shot and quite another to know full well that you can do it again at the next opportunity.

36

THE GUNNER'S GRAIL

We call it a "double." It's a matter of killing two birds with consecutive shots, and it is possibly the most satisfying thing that a hunter can do with a gun.

Two birds, two shots is, of course, the loosest definition—and because a double is the crowning achievement of game shooting, it's hardly surprising that all sorts of rational gymnastics have been applied in suggesting what might qualify. The late Charley Dickey wrote an essay years ago exploring the permutations of this, a piece as puckishly funny as only Charley could be. I can't remember them all, but my favorite is the "interrupted double"— killing the last bird you shoot at on one hunt and the first bird you shoot at on the next.

Sophistry aside, though, I believe the definition of a double truly does admit some latitude.

By the strictest account, it means two birds dead in the air at the same time. It does not, on the other hand, apply to killing two birds with a single

---

shot, the so-called "Scotch double." Shoot long enough and that kind of fluke will happen; it's happened to me with quail, doves, ducks, and prairie chickens. (The really weird part is that in the 45 years I've been a quail hunter, I've killed two bobs with one shot exactly twice—and both instances happened the same day, not ten minutes apart.) Suffice it to say that I've had a lot more double scotches on purpose than Scotch doubles by accident—and I've never once shot a Scotch double on birds by design.

Define it however you wish, but to me a double means taking a right and left—or under and over, two shucks on the slide, two pulls on the trigger, whatever—without appreciable delay between them. If I have time to reload, I can't call it a double. With doves, ducks, quail, prairie grouse, chukars, ptarmigan, or gray partridge, having two birds flying at once isn't at all unusual. It happens fairly often with pheasants, too. A genuine double flush of woodcock or ruffed grouse is a rare and lovely thing. More often, the second takes off at the sound of the gun or just before, but kill them both and I'm certainly willing to call it a bona fide double and stand the first round of drinks in congratulation.

Opportunities for doubles on driven game are commonplace, and if you make the shots you can get even the most jaded, blasé loader almighty excited. Gunning driven pheasants in Hungary a couple of years ago, I got lucky and shot seven straight doubles at the beginning of one drive; I thought my loader was going to kiss me. I've seen South American and Mexican bird boys literally jump up and down over a respectable string of doubles. Even English loaders, staid by nature, are apt to lose their heads and blurt out, "I say, well done!" when you take down a couple of clean rights and lefts. The double truly is the gunner's grail.

So why don't we do it more often? Why, in fact, don't we kill doubles nearly every time we have a good opportunity?

Judging from my own experience, and having watched a lot of other people shoot, it seems to me that we miss our second shots more often than our first. If you miss with the first barrel, rushing the shot is almost always the culprit. When it happens, forget about it, and go after the same bird with the second barrel. By then you're likely to be highly focused on that bird, and you've already built up at least some semblance of momentum in its direction. The same applies to shooting pairs in sporting clays: If you miss the first target, shoot at it again. You are statistically more likely to break it with the second shot than you are to hit the other target if you try to change focus. Fifty percent is always better than zilch.

Centering the first bird and missing the second is everyone's nemesis, and the usual suspect there is aiming. Smoke the first one and you're halfway to a double—but let that thought even flicker in your mind and you'll aim at the second, look at the gun in an effort to be ultra-precise, stop your swing, and shoot behind. I've done it many times, and I'll bet you have, too.

Every beginning skeet shooter thinks the doubles are a diabolic invention, and every old-timer offers the same remedy: Shoot the doubles as if they were two singles. It is an excellent piece of advice.

My father was a brilliant shot, at his best on quail, and if he told me once, he told me a hundred times that you flush quail by the covey but you have to shoot them one at a time. His main point was to caution me against flock-shooting, but it certainly applies to doubles as well.

Beginners go wrong at skeet doubles by thinking about the second target before they shoot the first and by trying to keep an eye on both at the same time—and thereby combine errors of poor timing and lack of focus. Clay shooters often make a similar mistake on pairs; try to watch both targets at once and the chances are excellent that you'll shoot right between them and not hit either one.

Bird hunters often come to ruin for the same reasons. If two or three or a whole covey of birds all get up at the same time, it takes some effort and discipline to pick out just one. The second shot will also be longer than the first. Knowing this, a gunner is under massive temptation to hurry the first shot and aim the second, thus applying too little focus on the one and the wrong kind of focus on the other. Even if he hits the first bird, the sight of the second one growing rapidly smaller with distance triggers an impulse to bear down and try to be oh-so-precise.

Now there are several things you can do to promote an effective second shot. One is to trust your gun. Most of us prefer to have one barrel choked a bit more tightly than the other. We do this in order to have the same pattern spread and density at thirty yards that we have at twenty—and that being the case, there's no need to be any more precise with the second shot than with the first. Just let the gun do what it's set up to do, and don't try to second-guess it.

The real key, however, is technique, and this harkens back to the skeet-shooter's advice I mentioned earlier: Don't think of two birds in the air as a double; think of them as two singles—but more to the point, shoot them as if they were two singles. If you can make one good shot, you can make two, *provided you make them as nearly identical as you possibly can.*

Keeping the basic elements of technique intact from one shot to the next is crucial. I can't tell you how often I've seen gunners do everything right with the first barrel and everything wrong with the second. The reason, I suspect, is a little panic attack, a momentary fear that there's just no time to do anything but fling a Hail Mary shot at a rapidly escaping target. Sometimes the second bird really is too far gone, and the best thing you can do is save the shell. More often, though, you have a lot more time to make a good second shot than you might think.

Let's say you've just killed a bird on a covey rise with the first barrel and there are others still flushing or still within reasonable range. The first thing that needs to move are your eyes.

Watch a beginner trying to shoot skeet doubles, and chances are you'll see him start swinging the gun at the second target while he's still watching the first either break or fly on. This isn't quite as heinous a sin in skeet, because you know where the second target is, more or less, and you know where it's going. Birds, on the other hand, can go anywhere they want and they don't tell you beforehand, so if you start moving the gun before you've focused on a target, it is motion without purpose and therefore more likely to work against you than in aid of the next shot.

But if you move your eyes first, look for and focus on the second target, then you've initiated eye-hand coordination in proper sequence. Where the eye goes, the hand will follow and will do so with wonderful accuracy. Try this right now: Look at something across the room, and then point your finger at it. Easy, right? There's no wasted motion and you're pointing exactly where you look. But try pointing at something you're not focused on, something at the outer edge of your peripheral vision, and then look to see how close you've come.

Move your eyes first, always.

And while you're picking out a new target, you should be re-mounting the gun. If you've had any coaching at sporting clays, I imagine you've been told that the best way to shoot following or report pairs is to dismount the gun after the first shot and go back to the ready position in anticipation of the second target. It's good advice, because it helps you keep your technique consistent. It also applies, at least in abbreviated form, to true pairs, whether clays or birds.

You may have made a perfect mount on the first shot, snapped the stock right under your cheekbone, but after you pull the trigger, the gun won't be exactly where it was a moment before. Recoil has caused it to move, maybe only a little, maybe a lot, but the point is that you and the gun now are in a different physical relationship, and even if it was perfect before, it ain't perfect now.

Your inclination probably will be to scrunch down onto the gun, but you'll be far better off if you can resist that temptation and instead start the swing-and-mount sequence over again—not necessarily from the original ready position, but certainly in some way that duplicates the same core technique you used for the first shot.

The best way I've found of doing this effectively is to drop the gun away from my cheek and shoulder—just a couple of inches will do—and then push my leading hand toward the bird I've picked out. That gets the gun moving in the right place, and it allows me to bring the stock to my cheek just the way I did before.

From there, focus is everything. Keep your eyes locked onto the bird, stay loose and just swing the gun, pull the trigger, and trust that what worked once will work just as well a second time.

If I had to identify in a word the arch-enemy of the second shot, I'd say "effort." Too much effort wrecks your rhythm and timing, causes aiming, overrides the simplicity of instinctive shooting. Bryan Bilinski and I have a little trick we often play with our students on the high incoming target that's a standard part of our Fieldsport Wingshooting Schools. Once they've had some experience with the shot, we'll load two shells for them and tell them to fire the second if they miss with the first. It's really a set-up. What we're waiting for is a first-barrel hit that leaves a sizeable chip still in the air, and when it's there we'll say suddenly, "Shoot the piece!" Instinct takes over because there's no time to think, and the piece typically disappears in a puff of dust. It's a great way to demonstrate what sheer technique can do.

You can do the same thing in practice, but I don't really recommend shooting chips until you're comfortable with the remount. If you follow an indoor practice routine, you can extend it to include a second shot. Pick a line, swing on it, and when you've pulled the trigger—either literally or in your imagination—shift your eyes to some other spot, drop the gun slightly, and swing along the new line with a second mount.

You can do this as slowly as you need to in order to get a feel for it, until taking two shots is as familiar as taking one. Then shoot some skeet doubles, concentrating on making two smooth, instinctive swings, always focused on the target. Trap doubles are good, too, especially if you have the field to yourself and can safely move up right behind the trap house. Don't worry if you hit or miss; making a good move on each target is what you're after. Learn to do that and the hits will come.

At that point, you're ready for more demanding practice, and there's nothing better than shooting chips. They're smaller than whole targets, so you have to concentrate harder to get a good visual lock; they fly off at unpredictable angles, so you really have to go after them; and you can't dawdle around, so you have to rely solely on instinct, focus, and the fundamentals of technique.

When you finally take what you've learned to the field and apply it to the real thing, you'll be surprised at how deadly your second barrel has become—and pleased to find how attainable the gunner's grail really is.

37

PARALYSIS BY ANALYSIS

It's been a while since I drew one of my tediously extended parallels between golf and shooting, and much as I appreciate all the cards, letters, and other expressions of thanks for that, I'm going to ask you to bear with me through one more. There's a point to it.

Golf instructors encourage players to develop swing thoughts. A swing thought is something a golfer can focus upon as he sets up to the ball and thus exclude everything else that could be swarming through his mind. (I realize many are disinclined to believe that golfers have minds, but I'd rather not go there just now.) Suffice it to say that as he prepares to make contact with the ball, a golfer is subject to a bewildering array of things to think about—grip, stance, posture, the lie, the wind, his takeaway, swing plane, wrist angle, swing axis, transition from back to down, weight transfer, angle of the clubface, on and on and on, right down to fretting about who's watching. It's all too easy to become overwhelmed by such a barrage of distractions. When a player's head feels like a hundred tennis balls in a clothes dryer, the chances are good that he won't do anything right.

Hence the swing thought—one or two simple mental images a golfer can use to occupy his mind while allowing his muscle memory to perform without conscious direction. And by "simple," I mean truly that. I, for instance, have two favorites; at address, it's "smooth," to keep me from jerking or hitching on the backswing, and at the top it switches to "snap," reminding myself to start the clubhead down slowly and accelerate through contact as if snapping the club like a whip. The rest, good or bad, I leave to what kinetic memory I've developed through practice.

Although the act of swinging a gun and pulling the trigger on a target is infinitely less complicated than making a good swing with a golf club, shooters, too, are subject to mental overload, with much the same result. Some instructors call it paralysis by analysis, which pretty well describes what happens.

It may be simpler than a good golf swing, but a good gun swing still requires the integration of several different physical elements—and if you try to consciously supervise all of them at once, you'll end up controlling none of them. The brain momentarily short-circuits, and the nervous system responds with something that looks more like a convulsion than an athletic move. Or with paralysis. I've had students get into such a mental tizzy that they literally could not move the gun or pull the trigger.

What bedevils the shooter, or the golfer, into these conditions is exactly what Coleridge identifies as Hamlet's problem—"an excess of ratiocinative meditation." Which is to say he thinks too much. And the more he thinks, the less able he is to act. Paralysis by analysis. I'm not sure about killing your uncle, but it's perfectly okay to think about hitting a golf ball or a clay target or a game bird—until the time comes to actually do it. Then, the thinking must end and the action begin. If the thinking continues, the efficiency and effectiveness of the action will be impaired, because we simply are not equipped to perform complex actions while thinking complex thoughts.

Among the faculty of our shooting schools, we describe the Perfect Shooter as about nineteen years old, extremely fit, with excellent coordination, perfect vision, and an IQ of twelve. As our students typically are somewhat brighter than that, they usually have to go through an over-thinking period before we can lead them into the non-thinking stage. Even though the technique we teach comprises only five basic elements, they still at first represent five different things to think about, and the more unfamiliar someone is with the way we want him to handle a gun, the more thinking he has to do early on. That's okay; we expect it and approach the opening sessions in ways that help people become physically familiar with the various elements fairly quickly. The sooner their muscle memory begins to develop, the less they need to think about what they're doing.

Sometimes, though, there's a gulf between how much thinking they *have* to do and how much they're inclined to do. Certain people naturally tend toward a high level of analysis—either because they're beginning to understand the implications of what we're asking them to do, or else it's just their nature to think things half to death. Though we encourage everyone to develop swing thoughts, the hyper-thinkers are the ones who can benefit most from finding a way to put their minds in neutral.

The set-up in shooting is just like the set-up in golf; shooting clays, you can take all the time you need to get your stance, posture, and ready position in place before calling for the target. But at that point, just before you say "pull," the swing thought needs to take over and everything else needs to go out the window.

Helping someone accomplish this requires both a bit of basic psychology and good observation. If you want someone to get something out of his mind, the worst thing you can do is tell him not to think about it—because it virtually assures that he *will* think about it. The effective approach is to put into his mind something you *do* want him to focus on, something that will be of most benefit in accomplishing what he's about to attempt.

What that might be varies from shooter to shooter. We look for the weakest element in each shooter's technique and try to make that his primary focus in a positive way. For an aimer, one who persists in looking at the gun instead of just the target, the best swing thought is "watch the target." For someone whose gun-mount is inconsistent, it's "to the cheek." For one whose visual focus on the target isn't as sharp as it could be, "leading edge" works very well.

And we don't merely offer these as suggestions. We hammer them again and again. It may be monotonous to sound like broken records, but it's effective. By standing behind the shooter and, when the target's in the air, repeating into his ear the thought we're trying to instill—"leading edge, leading edge, look at the front, look at the front"—we can usually plant that thought firmly in a fairly short time.

Occasionally, a shooter finds this distracting—but that tells us he's still overthinking, that what he's being distracted from is not what we're telling him to focus on, but rather some other stray thoughts that we're trying to get him to discard. In that case, we back up, review all the basics, and then start leading him once again to the main focus we want.

Now and then, we'll implant a swing thought that isn't specific. We do this with shooters whose technique is fundamentally sound but who want to spend five minutes analyzing every shot after they've taken it, and thus have to regain their focus before they take the next one. We let them do this a few times, because they're clearly enjoying their new-found understanding of the method, but then put a clamp on it. We can analyze to our heart's content between sessions, but right now, the task is to build muscle memory by actually moving the gun and pulling the trigger. My favorite swing thought in this situation is "just shoot the ****in' thing." Being unexpected, it usually strikes them as sufficiently funny that it sticks.

Clay shooters especially need good swing thoughts. The current trend among course designers is to find ways of playing with your head—optical illusions, targets with highly complex flight lines, awkward angles, that sort of thing. If you shoot clays as a means of keeping your field shooting polished, you're better off avoiding such silliness and seeking out the truly birdlike presentations. But if you shoot clays for its own sake, you'll have to find ways of getting your mind focused despite the presentation's attempt at scrambling your brain. And you may have to find a different focus for each different shot.

The first step is to study the target, ignoring as best you can everything extraneous—terrain, background, impediments such as trees and shrubs, everything that isn't part of the target's actual flight path. If it's possible to go stand behind the trap and watch them fly, you can sometimes find revelations—falling targets that from the shooter's perspective appear to be rising, or vice versa. At any rate, the better your grasp of what a target is actually doing, the better your chance of hitting it.

Once you decide where you're going to take the shot, try to find the simplest thought that will help you get the gun to where the target will be a moment after you pull the trigger. It could be something like "down and through" or "up and ahead." Or you might identify the target's leading edge as a position on a clock-face—eleven, two, five, six-thirty, whatever helps you key in on what part of the target is actually leading the way to where it's going. With what the hotshot clay shooters are now calling "transitional" targets—that is, targets that describe complex arcs and loops and curls—the leading edge is continually changing. If it's at three o'clock at one point, it might be at five o'clock twenty feet farther on, so find your best break-point, take a reading from the dial, and keep your timing consistent.

Bird hunters can use swing thoughts, too. I'd venture to say that the shots every hunter remembers best are the ones when a bird took him by surprise and he reacted from pure instinct, simply swinging and shooting without being aware of anything but the bird itself. On the other hand, I suspect we can all remember times when the dog was on point right out in the open, when we set ourselves into position to make a gimme shot—and missed with both barrels.

The more time we have to think, the more likely we are to think, analyze, plot, and plan. But if the mental gymnastics are still going on when the bird flushes, it's probably going to escape. That's when we're most apt to look at the gun, just to be a little extra-precise and make this easy shot perfect. It doesn't work. The more time you have to prepare, the more you need to get your swing thought in place and let it wipe out everything else. Repeat it over and over in your mind as you walk in on a point or watch a dove or a duck fly in from half a mile away. Get in the habit, and you'll miss fewer easy shots—and hit more difficult ones as well.

What you choose as a favorite swing thought is up to you, but it'll be most effective if it's something that either helps sharpen up a weak spot in your technique ("slow and smooth" for someone who is often too quick and jerky) or gets your attention where it ought to be ("look for the head"). If all else fails, try mine, and just shoot the effin' thing. It works often enough to keep me happy.

38

APPLES AND ONIONS

$\mathbf{B}$eing a teacher myself, the quality of instruction available to shooters is a particular issue with me. I've been a student to quite a few instructors and an instructor to a lot of students. I've worked with and watched some teachers whose incompetence makes me cringe and with some others whose skill I admire immensely. The whole experience has left me convinced that poor teaching is worse than none at all.

But how is the new shooter—or the veteran shooter new to instruction—to tell the difference? Sometimes it's not easy to know, even after the fact, whether the instruction you've had is going to do you good or ill in the long term, so it's no wonder people often feel as if they're flying blind on the front end of things.

In most instructional fields, certification is meaningful. If you sign up for flying lessons with a certified flight instructor, or for golf lessons from a PGA teaching pro, you can be assured that he or she is competent in the technical aspects of what you're out to learn. Not so in shooting. Certification in and of itself is all but meaningless.

I haven't paid a lot of attention to this sort of thing, but I know certain organizations certify instructors at certain levels. The question is, certified by whom and on what basis? As I understand it, these "certifications" are given by people already "certified" and that those certified beyond a certain level are able to certify others at the entry level. Moreover, I'm told the levels are based solely on the number of lessons someone has given.

In short, it would seem that the whole matter of certification is a self-perpetuating system in which advancement is determined by quantity rather than quality. If the first certifier in the chain doesn't know his butt from a hot rock about teaching, then the whole system is flawed—and even if he's a wizard, there's no assurance that his high-level underlings are any good at it if they got where they are solely by dint of numbers. Some people can do something a zillion times over and never get any better than they were the first time.

Now, this isn't to say that a "certified" instructor can't be a good one. I know some who're great. But it is to say that certification itself is no assurance. If an instructor is good, he's good, certified or not, and the converse is also true. (I'm using the masculine pronoun here because that's the convention of our language and because the majority of shooting instructors are men—but there are some women in the field who are first-rate teachers.)

Along the same line, don't assume that someone is a good instructor just because he's a good shot. The silly cliché "Those who can, do, and those who can't, teach" was coined by someone who couldn't do either. Teaching is a skill entirely separate from performance. A lot of great performers, in anything, aren't worth a damn at teaching, partly because their natural ability is so great that they don't really known how they do what they do, and partly because their way is the only way they know.

A good teacher is not just someone who knows how to shoot; it's someone who knows how to teach people to shoot—and there's a huge difference between the two.

So we're back to the original question: How can you tell a good teacher from a bad one?

Reactions of former students are a good indicator, though not infallible. Find someone who's been through the school or had lessons from the teacher you're considering, and ask how he liked it. You have to keep in mind that some people confuse quality of instruction with their own ability to perform what they're taught; that their expectations may have been unrealistic; and that they, not their instructors, may have been the source of personality conflicts.

You can get around some of these by asking other questions: What were you taught? Was the instruction clear or confusing? Did the instructor make you feel comfortable or intimidated? Did he do much shooting by way of demonstration? How much have you practiced what you learned?

What you want to hear: The emphasis was on the fundamental elements of shooting technique. The instructor found ways of making things clear to me. I felt very comfortable. He did little or no shooting himself.

The question about practice will tell you something about expectations. Those who expect instruction alone to make them competent shots are unrealistic. Instruction provides the tools, but how well you learn to use them depends entirely on how much you practice.

What you don't want to hear: We spent little or no time on fundamental technique, and he talked mostly about how much to lead any given target. When there was something I didn't understand, the instructor just kept saying the same thing over and over. I was just as intimidated, or confused, at the end of the lesson as I was at the beginning. He did as much shooting as I did, or more.

These are all characteristics of an instructor who cops an I-know-how-to-do-this-and-you-don't attitude, and that's the sign of someone who doesn't know how to teach.

Fundamentals are everything, the irreducible basis of every athletic skill and the basis of how it should be taught. In my experience, at least ninety-eight percent of an expert-shot's problems (and all of those that afflict beginners) are traceable to some error in fundamental technique. Any instructor who doesn't focus there isn't giving you your money's worth.

And unless you're out to learn how to shoot high-gun, American-style skeet on the sustained-lead method, lead is utterly meaningless. Any instructor who harps on "lead" and constantly gives you prescriptions—two feet, four and a half feet, nine feet, whatever—is a lousy teacher.

A good teacher's presentation is well polished, but it's not the only song he knows. Although learning is a natural talent, not everyone learns in the same way, and teachers who can't adapt what they're trying to get across to the ways individual students learn aren't very good instructors, able to teach only what and how they were taught. They remind me of people who think they can communicate with people who don't speak English by speaking English louder.

If you're a beginner, you're likely to feel intimidated at the start of a lesson. If your instructor lets you stay that way or makes you feel even more intimidated as the lesson goes on, he's not somebody you want to see for a second session. It doesn't necessarily mean he's a bad teacher, but it does mean he's not a good match for you.

An instructor who teaches mostly by demonstration is not only one who knows just one song, he doesn't even know all the words. The point, after all, is to teach you to shoot, and you can learn that only when the gun's in your hands. If I'm dealing with a visual learner, I'll take the gun and show him what I want him to do—and with those who're very visual, I might fire a shot or two—but for the most part the only time I put my hands on the gun during a lesson is while the shooter is holding it, so he can get a clear sense of how proper gun movement feels.

It's seldom possible, but perhaps the best way of all to learn whether a teacher's right for you is to watch him give a lesson to someone else. An audit will tell you all the things I've talked about, with the added benefit of being able to look for the dead giveaways to a poor instructor—watching targets instead of watching his student shoot targets; allowing errors in basic technique to go uncorrected as long as a shot results in a hit; telling the student what he did wrong without offering a clear, simple suggestion on how to do it right; and assuming every miss to be an error.

Sometimes we just miss, despite the best execution of technique. It might be a matter of moving the gun barrel an inch too much or too little. Students who come with the notion that success means hitting every last target are sometimes nonplussed when I tell them they made a good shot on a target they missed, but the art of shooting flying is inexact, and letting them think otherwise is a disservice.

And while we're on the matter of expectation, you should also understand that in order to be optimally effective, the form of instruction you take ought to fit your need. If you're a beginner or don't have a sound method grooved into muscle memory, you can't expect to learn an entire technique in a single lesson. You need a full-fledged shooting school for that; single lessons are most valuable for refining or working kinks out of what you already know.

This is true of learning almost anything. When I decided to take up golf again, I went through a series of lessons in order to develop an integrated technique. This summer, I found myself having difficulty hitting irons well, and after asking around to find the best teacher in these parts, spent an hour with Gary Metzger in Rapid City. He watched me hit a few shots and asked me to change the position of the ball in my stance, watched a few more shots and asked me to flatten my wrists a bit at the top of the back-swing and to start rolling them sooner on the downswing. That and enough practice to commit those moves to kinetic memory did the trick.

Some important points here. In each case, the scope of instruction was appropriate to what I needed to learn. In the series of lessons, Dave Cheatham helped me build a sound technique; in the single session, Gary gave me specific suggestions, all part of fundamental technique, meant to solve a specific problem. That's good teaching, and the same concept applies to shooting. Everything, success and problems alike, stems from the basics.

One of the enduring myths about instruction in anything is that in-eptitude does beginners no harm—in this case, that a teacher who can't help an expert shot is still okay for a beginner. On the contrary, it seems to me that everyone needs a good teacher, and especially beginners. There's just no substitute for a good start, and a good start can only happen with a good instructor.

An apple for the teacher is an old tradition that I'm sure was brought here from Europe. It was originally meant as a bribe, but I'd like to think of it as a reward for a job well done. Every good teacher deserves one. Those who approach teaching on the waves of an ego trip deserve something else.

39

STEADY TO FLUSH

It's taken me a while to find them, but there really are some good things that come about as we grow older. Some are mainly compensatory—optometry can usually mitigate failing eyesight, and even if audiology can't do much for shooter's ear, less-than-perfect hearing is not entirely without reward. In a few instances, though, being older truly is better than being younger.

My old friend John Madson first pointed this out to me over a campfire and some good whiskey one night years ago. John felt he was a better shot then than he'd ever been in his youth—and not just because he'd had more years to practice. What age had stolen from his youthful reflexes, he said, was replaced by a level of poise that made speedy reactions unnecessary. Or as he actually put it, he had grown steady to flush, no longer rattled by the sudden explosion of wings.

He proved his point not long after, on a Kansas roadside, rummaging happily in the back of his pickup for shells and declaiming loudly on the need for silence and stealth, while the rest of us watched about three hundred pheasants blow out of the ditches all around. He closed the tailgate with a slam that may have rattled windows in Wichita but certainly flushed one last rooster—upon which John turned, slicked a round into the chamber of his 16-bore Model 12, and killed it stone dead at about fifty yards. Then he flashed a grin that could etch glass and said, "I figured there'd be a bird here somewhere. How come you guys didn't shoot?"

Having reached the age now that John was then, I know exactly what he meant. I don't fire nearly as many cartridges in a year's time as I used to, mainly because I don't shoot targets nearly as much—and yet I shoot better now than I ever have. I believe I've finally become steady to flush.

I'd like to think this is the product of innately graceful skill burnished to a high lustre by maturity, but what I'd like to think and what those who know me would agree with are likely to be distinctly different. Fact is, I don't know exactly how I got to where I seem to be. I suspect through a combination of time and experience—though some of my friends have suggested that I've reached a level of obliviousness sufficient to make me steady to an exploding hand grenade.

In any case, this matter has been on my mind for some time. Bryan Bilinski and I have been kicking around the notion of collaborating in an instructional video on advanced shooting technique. We've each made films on the fundamentals, and given the teaching we've done together over the past few years, taking it all a step further seems only natural.

But it raises a basic question: What's the difference between shooting and advanced shooting? What is it that enables a shooter who has a sound, consistent technique to achieve the next level of skill?

The only answer we've come up with so far that makes sense is poise. Being, in other words, steady to flush.

When the physical game reaches a certain plane, the emphasis shifts to the head game. I'm not going to inflict any extended metaphor on you here, but I can't think of a better example of this than golf. The difference between a top-notch amateur and a Tour pro is not in the swing. Mastery of technique is entrée to the mini-tours, but what allows a player to move successfully from there to the big show is not what happens between his hands, but rather what happens between his ears.

In golf as in other physically demanding sports, the window of opportunity is relatively narrow, and a well-developed head game has to coincide with the time when physical capacities are at their peak. This can only be accomplished through complete immersion in the game. If such young lions as David Duval and Tiger Woods had to hold down day jobs in order to support themselves, they would not play as brilliantly as they do.

We as shooters have an advantage over golfers in that our sport is not as physically strenuous, that our window is much broader, and that perfection is always attainable. This is especially true in game shooting. Grinding out several hundred targets at a stretch in trap or skeet or clays is an exercise best performed by the young and fit, but game shooting isn't nearly so demanding.

For golfers, par is the standard to play against, and there aren't many limits on how much that standard can be bettered, especially over the four-day stretch of a professional tournament. Nowadays, a winning score that isn't double digits under par means a monster of a course or miserable weather or both.

For game shooters, par is perfection. It simply means hitting what you shoot at—and we are not required to fire at every bird we see. We can be perfectly successful without having to consistently drive a golf ball 300 yards, play short irons with pinpoint accuracy, or putt a ball across an undulating green into a 4¼-inch hole. All we have to do is place a moving object of our choice somewhere inside a three-foot shot swarm and perfection is ours. And there is, moreover, no particular number of times we have to do it. Taking a limit with the same number of shots is as good as we can expect, but even if we come home with one bird for one cartridge fired, it's still perfect shooting. It's possible to do better, to scratch down two birds with one shot, but that's a fluke.

And because most of us are, or will be, capable of swinging and firing a gun well into our seventies or eighties, we don't have to resort to total immersion in order to reach advanced stages of skill.

But we do, I believe, have to become steady to flush, have to become immune to being rattled by a flushing bird, have to reach a level of repose in which we can make our haste slowly and with purpose.

One of my favorite scenes in Clint Eastwood's masterpiece movie, Unforgiven, has the sheriff, a seasoned gunfighter, explaining things to the greenhorn Eastern journalist. You don't have to be faster than the other guy, says Little Bill, because the other guy is likely to get rattled and rush himself. Better to shoot only as fast as you can shoot and hit anything.

"But what if the other guy doesn't get rattled?" the tinhorn asks.

"Then he'll kill you, sure as hell."

Although it's clearly to our advantage that game birds don't shoot back, the concept is sound: Get rattled and you'll probably miss. Stay calm and your shot will more than likely count. Learn to be steady to flush and your level of shooting will noticeably advance.

What birds do that rattle us is partly what makes them game. They attempt to escape, as quickly and effectively as they can. They may rely on speed, maneuverability, and the chaotic advantage of numbers, but it's all an attempt to escape, and they're very good at it in their own ways.

It seems to me that being steady to flush involves two aspects. One is practicing the simple concept of not shooting at everything that flies. Years ago, one of my father's hunting partners, who was not a very good shot, commented on every miss by saying, "Well, you gotta get the lead in the air." As a kid, I must've heard him say it a thousand times. It's obviously true, but only up to a point. Lead in the air is useless unless it stands a high likelihood of connecting with what you're trying to hit. It's not worth a damn at birds that flush too far away or otherwise offer nearly impossible shots.

A moment of evaluation is worth any amount of lead in the air. Any but the rankest beginner can tell in an instant which birds he's likely to hit and which shots will depend on sheer luck. Don't kid yourself. Be deliberate, pick your shots, and pass up the rest. It's good conservation, and it's an excellent step toward advancing your skills. Making focus and evaluation your initial response will do a great deal toward short-circuiting the panic reaction.

That's the other element in developing poise—keeping your head while the birds lose theirs. Perhaps this seems too elementary to mention, but think for a moment. We've all encountered some wild animal under circumstances when both parties are startled. The beastie could be anything from a sparrow to a black bear, but the result is a demonstration of Newton's third law—you startle the bejeezus out of each other and leap in opposite directions.

Unfortunately, that's how shooters often react to flushing birds. The response is one of alarm rather than fright, but the result is the same.

The bird takes off in a headlong rush to save its skin, and the shooter flails about just as desperately, panicky that it's going to disappear before he can get off a shot. Under the circumstances, getting the shot off is about all that happens.

The fact is, most flushing birds don't disappear all that quickly. Woodland game—grouse and woodcock—sometimes do, but that's a function of environment rather than the actual capabilities of the birds. A flushing grouse or pheasant or covey of quail can set up a dreadful racket, but all the thrashing and the noise does not necessarily translate to speed. Their top speed may be substantial, but their rate of acceleration is not. I can't tell you how many times I've blown away two useless shots before the bird has traveled thirty feet. It's amazing how they slow down when your gun is empty.

This is where "steady to flush" becomes a literal concept. It takes restraint to keep from slamming the gun to your shoulder at the first sound of wings, takes a measure of clear-headedness to remember that no bird alive can fly faster than a shot swarm, and takes a degree of faith to rely on the fact that almost any bird is actually more killable at twenty yards than at ten. But if you maintain your poise, keep a cool head, and trust both your gun and your technique, you're halfway toward making an effective shot even before you start moving the gun.

All this, of course, is the head game, the aspect of shooting that proceeds from a thorough acquisition of technique.

It can be learned but not really taught. If we were having a lesson together, I could ask you to move your hand from here to there in a certain way, and you'd find it easy to do. But if I said I wanted you to clear your mind of everything except the leading edge of the target and especially not to think about how fast it seems to be getting away, your mind would immediately fill with images of escaping targets. That's the way our minds work, and why the old kid's game of challenging someone to spend a full minute not thinking of elephants is so maddening. Whatever you tell yourself not to think about inevitably takes over your consciousness.

I do not, therefore, have a prescription for poise, except to suggest that the more positive your focus, the less any negative elements can intrude. It may seem contradictory, but for us the best head game is a blank mind. The more intensely you can focus your eyes, the more sharply you're focusing your mind at the same time, and that makes everything slow down and extraneous elements fade to the background.

For my part, I try to focus on the bird's head, for the same reason I try to focus on the leading edge of a clay target. It doesn't work every time, of course, but it works often enough, and when it happens, I'm not aware of anything except the bird. In fact, several times hunting quail this season I found myself so sharply focused on one bird that I was surprised when my companions told me that two or even three had flushed my way. If they weren't close to the one I was looking at, I just didn't see them.

The feeling when this happens is one of complete calm. There's no sense of urgency nor of any need to hurry, only the certainty that all I have to do is point my leading hand where my eyes are looking. It's as if I have momentarily become a basilisk—that mythological reptile that can kill with its eyes.

It is, not surprisingly, a very good feeling. Making a successful shot always is, but in this case there is an additional comfort in having discovered that time is a giver as well as a taker-away, that there's something I can do much better on the far side of fifty than I could on the windy side of thirty. I don't know if it fully repudiates the notion that old dogs can't learn new tricks, but I do know that becoming steady to flush makes being an old dog very pleasant indeed.

DISTRACTIONS

Around noon yesterday I was bustling around my office barefoot and accidentally kicked a box that's sitting on the floor. Caught the corner with the little toe of my left foot and gave it one hell of a bash. (I'm writing this in mid-July, incidentally, if you're wondering about the barefoot part.) I was sure I'd broken it. I didn't, as it turns out, but it couldn't hurt any worse if I had. Great way to start an afternoon.

I stopped working about four o'clock and cast about for something to take my mind off my foot, which by then was aching like a tooth. Vicky was off riding with one of her old rodeo chums, so in the absence of adult supervision, I decided to play a round of golf.

It was all I could do to get a golf shoe on that foot, and walking nine holes was out of the question, so I rented a cart, did my pre-round stretches, and took a few tentative practice swings. Not very promising; no way I could take a really full swing because I just couldn't finish with my weight fully on the outside of my left foot, the way you're supposed to.

I'm sure I was a sight, hobbling around like a three-legged moose, using whatever club I had in hand as a cane. I had to set the parking brake with my right foot because it hurt too much to push that hard with my left. But I birdied the first hole, just missed a par putt on the second, lipped out a birdie putt on the third, and it went that way for six more holes. I won't bore you with the details, but it was the best round of golf I've played in a month; I hit every fairway and all but three greens in regulation, finished three over par, which could as easily have been two over because my par putt on No. 9 stopped an inch short of the cup.

Does this, you're wondering, have anything at all to do with shooting? Actually, it does, because it illustrates the value of distraction.

When a beginning golfer sets up to the ball, his mind is swarming with dozens of instructions that he's trying to remember all at once. A Tour pro's mind, on the other hand, is clear of everything except one or two key swing thoughts, whatever he uses as a point of focus that allows his body to perform an act he's rehearsed a gazillion times, without any interference from his conscious mind. The beginner's on overload, the veteran's on auto-pilot.

This happens in shooting, too. In the shooting schools Bryan Bilinski and I teach, the beginners are overwhelmed at the end of the first day. Even the very simple method we teach seems bewilderingly complicated at first. But these are two-day schools, and by the end of the second day, it's all starting to come together for them. They've shot enough by then to develop some muscle memory, so they're losing the feeling of trying to remember too many things at once. And if they do as we suggest and practice a lot over the following weeks, the whole thing will grow progressively simpler. The ultimate goal is to reach a level where all they have to do is look at the target and point the gun.

Good shooters, like good golfers, have swing thoughts, too, and the better able they are to rid their minds of everything else, the better they shoot. You can analyze a target just as a golfer analyzes a fairway or a green, and that's fine—but once you've made up your mind, you need to suspend the thinking process and clear your head of everything but the key thought that works best for you. "Look—point" does it for me, because it gets me focused on the two most important elements of shooting—visual concentration on the target and pointing the gun as if pointing a finger. The rest of it—foot position, posture, the swing-and-mount movement—is so deeply ingrained in kinetic memory that I don't have to think about it.

But of course, I sometimes do think about it, and when that happens I usually end up missing shots I shouldn't miss. Being consistently able to clear your mind before you start moving the gun is easier said than done, but that's where a bit of distraction can help.

Looking back on yesterday's game, it's clear to me that the distraction of a nearly broken toe did something for me. I was hyper-aware of not over-swinging the club, which is every golfer's nemesis, because I knew it'd hurt like bloody hell if I did. So, my sole objective was to make a shorter swing and contact the ball crisply, and it worked.

Not all distractions are good. Thinking about the last shot you missed is an almost-certain ticket to missing the next one, too. Miss three or four and you'll be distracted to a fare-thee-well. The natural response is to bear down and try to be ultra-precise, start measuring, looking back and forth between the gun and the bird, tense up our gun-handling muscles, and so on—all of which are exactly the wrong things to do. Instead, you need to be loose and relaxed and focused solely on the target, never on the gun, so unless you can replace a negative distraction with a more productive one, you're likely in for a very bad day.

Relaxing is the first step. Find a log to sit on or a fencepost to lean against. Take five or six slow, deep breaths, concentrating on the sensation of breathing in through one nostril and out through the other. It's an old pre-meditation technique. You'll be surprised at how the tension drains away. Give yourself at least a twenty-minute break, and do something you find pleasant—smoke your pipe, eat a candy bar, drink some water, whatever.

When you start out again, don't let yourself tense up in anticipation of the next bird. It's useless to simply tell yourself not to think about something; doing so only ensures that whatever you're trying to avoid will be the only thing in your mind. Nature abhors a vacuum, so you have to replace negative thoughts with positive, or at least neutral, ones.

Talking to your partner is a great distraction—as long as you aren't talking about how lousy your shooting is today. If you're hunting alone, talk to your dog or talk to yourself, hum a tune, whistle a tune, try to recite something you memorized in high school, get your mind off shooting.

Hunting quail in South Texas with some friends last fall, I was out one afternoon with David and Maurer Culpepper (of the N'Awlins

Culpeppers). David was on one side of a strip of mesquite and black brush, Maurer and I on the other, walking along and talking about something. A single bobwhite popped up, went buzzing down the strip, and I shot it. Maurer gave me a quizzical look.

"I've never seen anybody move that fast." she said.

"Did I shoot fast?"

"The bird was dead before I got my gun halfway up."

Couldn't prove it by me. It was a completely instinctive reaction. I wasn't thinking about shooting, only about the conversation we were having. I don't even remember consciously having my Look–Point swing thought. It's a good example of how quickly and accurately we can perform a familiar move when our minds aren't getting in the way.

Some situations call for draconian measures. I once gave a lesson to a chap who was having a beastly time. The more he dwelt on it, the worse it got, and being self-conscious about shooting badly in front of someone didn't help, either. He'd worked himself into such a tizzy that just taking a break and talking about something else couldn't do the trick. The moment he got his gun in his hands, he fell right back into the grips of his misery.

Finally, I asked him to take off his left shoe, dropped a good-sized pebble into it and had him scrunch it around till it was right under the ball of his foot. We were on a skeet field, and I made a pretense of wanting to change the angle of the shot, so we walked to the other side; then I pretended to change my mind and we went back where we'd been—all of which was to make him keenly aware that he had a stone in his shoe.

Then I had him set up for the target with a cartridge case under his right heel, which put even more weight than usual on his leading foot. After a few minutes, he got distracted enough by the discomfort to start shooting without thinking about it, and as soon as he started hitting targets, his confidence came back. I suggested he keep the rock as a lucky charm and use it again if he needed to.

The bird season may be open when you read this, and maybe something here will help you over a rough patch in your shooting. For my part, me wee toe doesn't hurt quite as much as it did last night, though it's impressively swollen and, along with most of the top of my foot, a rather intense shade of purple. I'm truly amazed I didn't break it. I imagine it'll heal up in a few days, and I intend to play as much golf as I possibly can

---

before it does. After that, I dunno—I'm thinking about carrying a hammer in my golf bag and whacking a toe before every round. Might just do my game some good.

(41)

PANIC

Stress is a killer. Or so they tell us—and for a change I agree with whomever "they" happen to be. Having survived one heart attack and an ongoing battle with arrhythmia, both brought about by stress, I'm willing to concede the point. The cardiologists can have the high ground; from down here in the trenches, I can tell you that stress does kill good shooting.

Stress breeds panic, and panic spells the difference between a well-taken shot and a frantic, aimless poke.

Panic is by definition the sudden onset of powerful emotion, powerful enough to cloud your brain against a positive response. The behaviorists suggest—rightly, I believe—that under stress we revert to the most familiar response, whatever it is. That's why we tend to swear, count, and pray in the first language we learned. Reversion itself is neither good nor bad, simply a fact. The results, however, may be right or wrong, depending upon what we're trying to accomplish and what we revert to. In shooting, I notice, reversion usually goes wrong.

In teaching for twenty-odd years, I've asked myself time and again what causes reversionary panic among shooters. Where lies the stress? The only answer that makes any sense is the simplest one: Stress originates in either the anticipation or the sight of some object flying through the air.

Ever see a golfer make two lovely practice swings and then lunge at the ball as if trying to fell a ten-inch tree with one stroke of the axe? I have, and I've done it more often than I like to admit. We carefully coach our shooting school students in how we want them to swing and mount a gun—but put a target in the air, and the coaching often goes right out the window. The target introduces stress, stress breeds panic, and the wheels come off. The same guy who an hour earlier could execute a calm, beautifully integrated swing and mount suddenly looks like a man under attack by a swarm of bees. He snatches the gun to his shoulder, bangs his head down onto the stock, and then goes racing off after a target he thinks is going to disappear at warp speed any second.

The good part is, this is exactly what we instructors expect, and it's our entrée to the psychological aspect of the program. We leave it unspoken, never tell people ahead of time that we're going to play with their heads, but that's what we do. Through an unrelenting emphasis upon technique, we seek to demystify moving objects.

What we don't do is remove the stress. Not all stress is bad. Stress is an invitation to focus, and in the case of a flying target, focus is what we want. Stress becomes destructive when we lack the means to deal with it—when, in other words, we respond with panic rather than a workable plan. The plan is the essence of our message. We are purveyors of tools, peddlers of a simple technique that anyone can use to overcome the stress induced by a flying object. If we could expand this into concrete ways of dealing with the stresses of life in general, we could all go out on the inspirational-speaking circuit and become gazillionaires—and then go back to being shooting instructors, which is what we really love to be.

Enough of theory. I've written about technique *ad nauseum*, and I'm not going to rehearse it now. What I will say is that there are ways of playing with your own head that can help keep panic at arm's length.

Not to sound like some crackpot homeopath, but deep breathing helps. If you're on a target range, draw in and exhale a couple of big ones before you ask for the target. A deep breath supplies more oxygen to your muscles, and blowing it out relaxes them. Relaxed muscles are more efficient than tense ones. Breathing out just before you shoot is something you can train yourself to do on a skeet field, trap range, or clays course. When you can do it instinctively, you'll do it in the field as well. You can develop a habit of making a little exhaling *whoof* as you focus your eyes on a flushing bird, even one that takes you by surprise. What you don't want is the panic response of gulping in a huge breath and holding it.

If you're on a target course and feel yourself tensing up, try the old Zen technique of breathing in through one nostril and out through the other. It sounds doofy, I know, and you don't really do it, but with a little practice you'll start believing you can and come to feel it. It's a relaxation trick that works in almost any situation, not just shooting.

Another thing you can do is to avoid tanking up on coffee before you go out to shoot. A major caffeine buzz sets your nervous system ajangle and makes you all the more susceptible to a panic attack.

Visualization is also a good hedge, one that has multiple benefits. This works especially well at clay targets. Skeet targets are utterly predictable, trap birds are random, but only within a narrow parameter, and you can always get a view target if you're first on the stand at a clays course. The trick is knowing what the target is going to do—which comes with experience, even if momentary—and then not watching your fellow shooters or their targets. Instead, gaze off into the distance, imagine a soothing scene (I like to envision the calm surface of a pond or lake), then imagine seeing yourself swinging on a target and breaking it, then hold that image in mind when it's your turn to shoot. It works, not just for shooting but for virtually any physical act; the better you can visualize yourself doing something, the easier it is to perform whatever you're out to do. Every sport psychologist I've talked with agrees that this is a useful fundamental approach, and it works for anything else. I once talked with a welder who told me he always visualized himself drawing a perfect bead—and he was damn good at what he did.

The best advice I can offer against panic attacks is simply this: Take your time. I don't mean you should shoot as if in the midst of a narcoleptic fit, only that lunging at any target is likely to cause a miss. Get a good visual lock first ('cause you can't hit what you can't see), and then move your gun smoothly up the flight line. You don't have to rush. No clay target or game bird can outfly a shot charge that's moving roughly 800 miles per hour.

Either one can give you a very narrow window of opportunity, but that's just the nature of the sport.

By the end of a two-day Fieldsport school, our clients mostly refer to me as Mister Slowdown, because that's my most frequent admonishment once they've grasped the basic technique. Very seldom have I felt a need to encourage anyone to speed up. I might tell them to pull the trigger sooner, but that's a matter of timing, not an invitation to flail away out of control. You can shoot quickly, and sometimes you have to, but hitting anything in the grips of panic is invariably an accident. Making haste slowly, and calmly, is always the better way.

(42)

UPPER
MANAGEMENT

Apply for advancement in just about any endeavor and you'll have to prove up on several counts. I have only a vague idea what this involves in business, but I do know what we look for in shooting schools. And I have a notion there's not that much difference.

A declaration of having thirty years' experience doesn't cut much ice There is a difference between thirty years of real experience and one year's experience repeated thirty times over. We've come time after time across self-styled "advanced" shooters so sloppy in the fundamentals that they barely qualify as beginners. Time spent doesn't necessarily equal time learned.

To be ready for advanced instruction presupposes a soundly competent grasp of the basics. If you can set your feet to a target, lean yourself into a shooter's posture with your weight forward and your chin dropped just enough to open the gate to an unobstructed pathway between a good ready position and your cheekbone ledge; if you can start moving the gun with

---

231

your leading hand and not go into a swivet about thinking of your shoulder first; if you can focus your vision on the leading edge of a target, not succumb to the temptation of aiming, and make a firm, crisp mount time and again while seeing only a sharp target pursued by a fuzzy gun—if you can do all that consistently, you probably are ready to kick things up a notch.

The connection here is clear. In shooting, as in business, advancement means management, learning or perfecting those skills that allow you to perform at a higher level of efficiency, of productivity, of the ability to accomplish the job at hand. The difference is that shooting allows no delegation. It's just you and the gun and the target, hit or miss, and you live with the results. Knowing what's required certainly affects the outcome.

One of the things we expect our advanced shooters to learn is to read. In business terms, this is to spot a trend, recognize where it came from, where it's going, and where to pick up on it with the best results. Reading targets can be easy or difficult, depending. A straight-line clay or a flushing quail are straightforward enough—see the flight line and swing the gun from where it was to where it is to where it's going to be. Nothing hard about that. See a more complex trend and the reading is more difficult—a long, curving dropper, a chandelle, or a woodcock twisting up through treetops or a snipe that seems to fly with one wing at a time. Here you're presented with both a reading problem and a decision to make. The reading involves more complicated lines—because you still have to figure out the connection between where it came from and where it's going to be when you take the shot. And then decide where you're going to pull the trigger and how you'll get there. A more complex target offers more choices. Read closely and you may find a flat spot that invites a simple swing-through; the distance may demand a pull-away, or the sheer loopiness may dictate sustained lead as the best choice. These all work under the right circumstances. One of the requirements of advanced shooting is knowing which is most effective at a given moment, and of course, knowing how to execute the move.

Both are part and parcel of our advanced program—and by the "our" and "we" I'm using here I mean my shooting school colleagues and me. We're of a mind on the objectives, and even though we may choose different approaches, the end result is the same. We never go into a teaching session without a plan. Neither should you, whether it's a round of clays or a day in the field. Adopt a plan, adapt it to circumstances, follow it through, and you'll feel a lot better at the end. You won't hit everything you shoot at, and you shouldn't expect to. Be realistic, expect progress rather than perfection, and you've set an attainable goal. What's wrong with being happy over three more targets or two more birds? Beats hell out of pounding yourself to dollrags because you didn't hit everything.

Golf coaches talk about managing a round or managing a course. Shooting is no different. Management doesn't mean altering presentations so they accommodate the strong points of your game. You can't change a golf course or a clays course or the random reactions of game birds. All you can do is adapt, and how well you do that is the measure of your success.

The first step on a clays course is reading the targets. Don't just give them a cursory glance and allow them to stay in your mind as intimidating streaks impossibly fast or impossibly distant. Focus hard on any moving object and it will appear to slow down. Learn to separate flight lines from environment. Course designers, both in clays and golf, are wonderfully clever at creating illusions with background, can make rising targets appear to be falling and vice versa. If you can recognize the trick, you're already a long way toward foiling it. There are ways of taking the mystery out of presentations. One is to stand right behind the trap and watch some targets. If you can't do that, you can stand behind the shooting box and use your gun barrels to identify the flight line. Hold your gun at arm's length—action open, of course—put the muzzles where the target first appears, and then adjust the tilt so the targets flies right along the rib. Putting a straight edge on the flight line lets you compare what the target's really doing with what the background tempts you to see. Classify both these tricks under Reading Skills.

Once you have a good read, put your own plan into action. First, pick the spot where the target appears most vulnerable. This is a matter of both instinct and experience, and it varies a bit from shooter to shooter. Shoot enough and you should start to see an especially killable place in any flight line, some spot where you can move on it aggressively rather than flailing away in pure reaction. Maybe there's a flat spot in the flight path or some place where a target seems to hang motionless, whatever. If you're out to kill it rather than just chase it, learn to find and capitalize on its vulnerabilities. Clay shooters usually call this killing zone the break point.

Having decided where to take the shot, you can set yourself up to it with your feet, so you can swing up to and past the break point without going off balance and having to dip a shoulder. Beginners too often set up to the trap, as if they were going to break a target right off the arm rather than in the kill zone. When they reach the zone, their lower bodies start impeding their upper bodies, and the whole swing comes to a grinding halt, leaving no choice but to drop a shoulder, flail with their arms, and essentially disintegrate what could have been a nicely compact move. You can count that target a miss before it ever flies.

Set up for the kill, set your muzzles on the line you know the target's going to follow, and then pivot your upper body back toward the trap, back to a hold point that will allow you sufficient time to move the gun smoothly, without rushing, up the target's path, pass it, and swing ahead. Remember that the various so-called "methods"—swing-though, pull-away, and sustained lead—are not separate methods at all, but rather variations on the same simple theme. They're all a matter of seeing a flight line and moving the gun with the target. Bringing the gun back down the path to a hold point is the shooter's equivalent of a golfer's backswing; the best results obtain from making back and forward moves along precisely the same line.

With your feet set and a hold point established, you should knit everything together by looking to the place where you first see the target clearly. This, too, varies among shooters. Some have the acuity to focus on a target right out of the trap. Most of us don't, so we have to find the spot where that moving object changes from a blur to something hard-edged and definable. You can't shoot what you can't see. Seeing is thus paramount in letting everything else come together.

Other management tools apply once a target is in the air. One is to take advantage of a stand that allows Full Use of the Gun. This, sometimes known as FUG, simply means you can take two shots at any target, whether a single or some form of pair. Everybody soon twigs on how to use two shots at a single, but a lot of shooters FUG themselves unmercifully at pairs. True pair, following, or report, the problem is the same: Miss the first one and the second becomes a management issue. Too often, the approach amounts to a panicky, aimless poke in which the shooter, suddenly wound tight as a banjo string, clutches the gun for dear life and tries to aim it like a rifle.

Bird hunters often do the same thing, but they at least have the advantage of staying focused on the same target. At worst, panic sets in, everything tightens up, and the second go is a tribute to ammunition makers. For myself, I've somehow learned to get mightily pissed off at a first-barrel miss, directed not toward myself but rather at the bird for having the audacity to elude my superlative shooting. The second shot is usually deadly—but only because I go about it the way I should have gone about things in the first place. I try not to think about that until later.

For clay shooters, missing the first target of a pair ought to have the same effect, though it often doesn't. Unless the one you just missed is diving into the brush or otherwise dropping out of sight, use your second shot to kill it rather than trying to suddenly refocus and reestablish a whole different shot. If you're out to count X's and O's at the end, ask yourself if you'd rather walk off a field owning fifty percent or slink away under zero. You're almost always better off staying with one target of a pair.

All this presupposes the fundamental question of management: What are you trying to manage?

There are tricks and tricks, but even taken together they do not amount to a quick fix that covers every situation. For a real fix you have to rely upon your technique and manage the one thing that will most often work against you—your emotions. This more than anything spells the difference between a truly advanced shot and a competent beginner. I've seen some truly good shots come apart under no more pressure than they put on themselves, under circumstances that had no inherent pressure built in. It may be as simple as getting steamed up over missing a couple of easy ones and allowing that to erode a fundamentally sound technique. The one that sticks in mind was some years ago, when a guy I know well and admire as a well-seasoned shot went completely to pieces during a fun shoot and performed like a man under attack by hornets in a flurry he should have aced. It was painful to watch, but instructive in the aftermath. He was still shaking with frustration when I went up and asked what went wrong.

All he could say was, "I couldn't touch the targets." Well, Jesus O'Leary. Touching a target, which is simply a visual confirmation that you're swinging on the flight line, is about as fundamental as it gets, especially with straight-on incomers that fly along just begging to be killed. The problem wasn't his technique; it was something in his head that momentarily blocked his ability to do what his body knew very well. Unfortunately, it's not uncommon.

We tell all our shooters, quite truthfully, that we can bring them within six inches of being world-class shots. All they have to do is honestly use the tools we give them. That last six inches is the space between their ears, and that's a territory we can only tease around the edges, hoping that something we say gets through.

When destructive emotion gets in the way, you surrender control. You're no longer managing your performance. Instead, it's managing you, and the result is not likely to be pretty. When you lose focus on the task at hand and allow some extraneous notion—say, what your Uncle Fred is going to think about your performance—you've gone instantly from being a manager to a managee, and you're probably not going to like where you end up. Nor will Uncle Fred. The best you can do is forget about him and play your own game.

I like drawing analogies between shooting and golf. The skills, both physical and mental, are much the same, even though golf is by far more difficult to execute consistently well. But watch even good players and you'll see most of them start to unravel in the face of pressure, real or imagined. The ability to stick to a game and trust in what they know they can do is often the difference. No accident that the Scots once nicknamed Ben Hogan The Wee Ice Mon. For more current practitioners, watch Vijay Singh, Ernie Els, Nick Price, and Fred Couples. They all play so unflappably as to make you laugh. But don't be fooled by such calm demeanor. They may look as if they're about to fall asleep on the course, but their résumés bespeak a hawk-eyed focus that the rest of us can only wonder at. They're living proof that you don't have to be an automaton or a standoffish prick in order to perform at the highest level.

You do, however, need to know where your attention ought to be and how to keep it there. Those are the keys to performance—perhaps simple to say, but never simple to accomplish. Don't let that put you off. Work constantly on your fundamentals and learn to slough off distracting emotions. Just remember that advanced shooting is achieved step by step, never in a quantum leap. Quantum leaps we save, and savor, for beginners. Getting beyond that means grinding it out shot by shot. It's hard work, and hard work can be frustrating, but put out the effort, and you'll end up where you want to be.

43

THE DANGER

It is axiomatic that the path to wing-shooting nirvana lies in a sound technique combined with a well-fitted, well-balanced gun that has a good trigger.

And it's absolutely true. Develop a good technique and commit it to kinetic memory; shoot a gun of appropriate size and dynamics that is fitted to point where you look; have the triggers adjusted to proper weight and crispness—the skies will open and you'll hear the music of the spheres.

I could easily romanticize my younger days, given the wealth of game in the Midwest during the 1950s and early '60s. We had it good, Dad and I and our compatriots—an abundance of quail, a plethora of pheasants, ducks, woodcock; whatever there was in our narrow sphere was there in rich numbers, ours for no greater price than five minutes' conversation at a farmer's back door.

It was wonderful, but to be honest with you, I wouldn't trade a lifetime of that for what I've known in the past twenty-odd years.

My sphere is broader now, for one thing. I am privileged to do for a living what I did back then solely at the behest of passion, so I get to go where

237

game is abundant, and there are still a lot of farmers and ranchers who'll say yes to a polite request.

The real difference, though, is that I can shoot a lot better now than I could in the old days.

I love the countryside and the dog work as much as ever—and I can measure that by the fact that my feeling for the land and the dogs and the promise of game once was enough to sustain my passion in the face of being no better than a mediocre shot, if even that good. As I said, it's easy to romanticize a time when fifteen-covey days were commonplace, but I have to admit that being a better shot would have made the whole thing sweeter. Our sport is, after all, a trinity of bird, dog, and gun. How well I shoot doesn't make the difference between a good day and a bad one, because it's way more complicated than that—but shooting is a key part of the deal, and if I want good performance from the birds and the dogs, then I should expect no less of myself.

When I was about 35 I decided I was going to become the best game shot I could be. Sporting clays did not exist in this country at the time, so I took up skeet—to the tune of about 5,000 targets a month, shooting virtually year-round. And I got pretty good at it, first in high-gun American style, then in low-gun International style. My game shooting improved.

I took lessons from Jack Mitchell, who gave me the technique I was looking for. I took instruction from Ken Davies, Dan Carlyle, Roland Wild, Chrissie Alexander-Davis, Holly Haggard, Gil Ash, Jon Hollinger, and others—and learned something useful from every one. I practiced incessantly, constantly analyzing technique. I had all my guns fitted and balanced, had the triggers tuned just so.

It took a few years, but in the end, through the combination of diligent work and suitable equipment, I became a competent shot—no Lord Ripon, mind you, but good enough to feel satisfied that I had accomplished what I set out to do. Knowing that I'm going to hit most of the reasonable shots I choose to take has made hunting just that much better.

Now, if I can do this, anyone can. I've seen some authentic natural shots, but I'm not one of them. I wasn't born knowing how to shoot. My native eye-hand coordination is no better than average. I may have developed my meager gift more strenuously, but that's something anyone can do. I see myself as living proof that good instruction, hard work, and a proper gun can make a significant difference.

But then there is The Danger.

The price you pay in time, effort, and money to reach and maintain a high level of skill isn't the end of it. There's a catch: Once you get there, you can't go back. The skill you've worked so hard to develop will not transfer indiscriminately—and you may not be aware of the box you're getting yourself into until you try to step out of it.

It's possible to reach a point where you can shoot reasonably well with just about any gun you pick up. During the years when I wrote the "Gun Review" column for *Shooting Sportsman*, I could do just that. One or two new guns came along every couple of months, and I shot them all, a lot. Some suited me better than others, but I managed to do okay with all of them, simply because I was fairly adept at adapting.

But in the years since I switched columns, I have seldom shot any guns other than my own, and then only for a few shots here and there. As a result, my ability to adapt has all but disappeared.

And I never realized it till this spring, when I spent two days with a mixed group of gun and automotive writers at an event co-sponsored by Holland & Holland and Land Rover—two days of shooting clays and quail with Holland's splendid guns and driving the remarkable Rovers both off-road and on. Tough duty, I know, but there was a bit of a shock hidden inside the fun, at least for me.

It started on the second field at the clays course. Holland's had a different gun on each stand, and this one was a magnificent Royal Ejector side-by-side. The stock was a wee bit too long and too high, but the target was a quartering incomer that I can normally grind up in my sleep. It's my favorite shot at doves and driven game, and I've practiced it endlessly.

After missing the first four, it was clear that, despite technique and an excellent pair of triggers, this gun did not shoot where I looked, and after four more flopped down unharmed in front of me, I still hadn't a clue where it actually was shooting. At that, I shook my head and handed it back to the puller.

"Wait a minute," he said. It was a ten-target format. "You're not finished."

A nod and a rueful laugh. "Oh, yes I am."

The rest of the round was, to put it mildly, uneven. Some guns I could shoot very well, some only marginally well, and some not at all. Why was obvious. The question in my mind was, Why can't I adjust the way I used to?

Next day we hunted plantation quail, and it was more of the same. With a 20-bore Royal over/under that felt very good, I missed two shots all morning. Because there weren't quite enough Holland guns to go around, I gave it to someone else in the afternoon and took one of the "extra" guns, a 12-gauge Ruger, instead. The fit was close enough, and I didn't mind the inherently barrel-heavy balance, though it's more pronounced than I like. But the trigger was hard as stone.

I don't mention this to pick on Ruger. Red Labels are well-made guns, but the factory-standard trigger pulls are awful. I know why they're the way they are, and I can't blame any manufacturer for wanting to avoid the idiotic morass of product-liability suits, but the fact remains that Ruger triggers are way too heavy and rough for good shooting—or at least they are to one who's spent years shooting with much lighter, much crisper pulls.

A heavy trigger causes a reaction similar to a flinch: You lurch forward, rolling your shoulder into the gun, trying to make it go off. When you do that, the muzzles drop and you lose momentum, so you miss low and behind. I did manage to kill a few quail with that gun, but not very many, and every shot was a struggle.

On the other hand, the opposite is also true where The Danger is concerned. Pulls more than about three ounces lighter than what I'm accustomed to give me a severe case of premature triggeration—which not only wrecks my shooting, but also scares the bejeezus out of me because of the safety hazard.

Narrow is the path, and strait is the gate.

Of course none of this is any argument against developing good technique or having guns that fit and shoot properly. On the contrary, that truly is the only route to becoming the best shot you can be. If you're content to be a so-so shot with virtually any gun, it's your choice to make. If you're not, just be aware that The Danger exists. You won't see it coming till it has you firmly in its clutches, and realizing that you've traded versatility for better performance can be frustrating, even embarrassing, at times.

About all you can do is look at it philosophically. If I've backed myself into a corner where I can only shoot at my best with my own guns, so be it. I worked hard to get here, and while it has turned out to be a tighter corner than I ever expected, it's still a sweet place to be.